This

Sandra Lee
semi-homemade®
slow cooker recipes 2

book belongs to:

....

Special thanks to Culinary Director Jeff Parker

Meredith® Books Des Moines, Iowa

Copyright © 2007 Sandra Lee Semi-Homemade® All rights reserved. Printed in the USA.

Library of Congress Control Number 2007929218 ISBN: 978-0-696-23815-4

Brand names identified in this book are suggestions only. The owners of such brand names retain all right, title, and interest in and to their respective brands. No manufacturers or brand name owners have endorsed this collection or any recipe in this collection.

P9-BYC-424

sem·i·home·made

adj. **1:** a stress-free solution-based formula that provides savvy shortcuts and affordable, timesaving tips for overextended do-it-yourself homemakers **2:** a quick and easy equation wherein 70% ready-made convenience products are added to 30% fresh ingredients with creative personal style, allowing homemakers to take 100% of the credit for something that looks, feels, or tastes homemade **3:** a foolproof resource for having it all—and having the time to enjoy it **4:** a method created by Sandra Lee for home, garden, crafts, beauty, food, fashion, and entertaining wherein everything looks, tastes, and feels as if it was made from scratch.

Solution-based **E**nterprise that **M**otivates, **I**nspires, and **H**elps **O**rganize and **M**anage time, while **E**nriching **M**odern life by **A**dding **D**ependable shortcuts **E**very day.

dedication

To the not so slow making Semi-Homemaker,
you deserve every wonderful day
to be filled with delicious food
and special moments.
I know this book will bring you
joy and happiness.
Always know that all
of your hard work is worth it!

Table of Contents

Chapter 1

One-Pot Meals
18

Chapter 2

Beans and Chili
46

Letter from Sandra

Last week, I had a few friends over. I greeted them with Chai Tea Toddies to help us unwind after a long day. For an entree, I served Chicken Scaloppini in a creamy wine sauce with a medley of tender spring vegetables. Dessert was simple—warm, crumbly Crème de Menthe Brownies with a scoop of French vanilla ice cream melting down the sides. My friends begged to know how I did it—especially on a weeknight after working all day. So I told them about my secret ingredient—the slow cooker.

The slow cooker is the solution to today's dinner dilemma: how to prepare delicious, well-balanced meals when time is short. This amazing low-tech convenience is your own personal chef—braising, baking, and boiling away while you're at work, the gym, or anywhere. But to make it even easier, the real secret is to cut down on your ingredients while stepping up the flavor. This is the Semi-Homemade® difference—while other recipes have long lists of ingredients, I streamline every one, using convenience products and little meat browning to save time without sacrificing taste or quality. It all adds up to my unique 70/30 philosophy: Mix 70% prepackaged supermarket foods with 30% fresh ingredients, toss in a dash of your own ingenuity and cook up something that's 100% fabulous.

I love to cook—I just have less and less time to actually do it. That's why I adore the concept of this book. You'll find a broad range of recipes, from classic favorites to nouvelle cuisine—all pulled together in minutes and slow cooked to perfection. You'll find fun meals to feed the family and chic starters that are perfect for parties. When it's comfort food you want, soups, chili, and pot roast offer traditional goodness with a splash of sophistication. For dessert, there's puddings, cobblers, cakes, and brownies, "baked" up moist, rich, and ready to enjoy.

Whether you're cooking the first course or the last one, the key ingredient is time. Semi-Homemade® plugs you in to the best of both worlds—dishes that are prepped fast and simmered slow, for a tender texture and a complex flourish of flavor that satisfies even the loftiest of expectations. Maximum flavor. Minimum fuss. Memorable meals. That's slow cooking the Semi-Homemade® way.

Cheers to a healthy, happy life!

Sandra Lee

Dinner Tonight;
Lunch Tomorrow

Too many leftovers to eat day after day? Just freeze them for a quick, easy-to-prepare meal a week—or month—from now. Divide the recipe into individual-size servings, wrap tightly, and label clearly. Then thaw, heat, and eat whenever you're hungry!

French dip sandwich made from leftover Roast Beef with Tomato Ragout (page 158)

Cincinnati-style chili from leftover Red-Eye Chili (page 56)

Dazzle Up Dinner

Here's the scenario: The pantry is sparse, the kids are hungry, and all you have to feed the family is leftover food from last night. But guess what? Nobody has to know! Reinvent last night's supper for a whole new meal the next day.

Second Time Around

Roast Beef with Tomato Ragout hit the spot on the first night, but can it continue its reign of glory on the second day? Yes! Give new life to this dish by using it for French dip sandwiches. Slice the roast beef, then pile it on hoagie buns with a bit of the remaining tomato ragout. Dip the sandwiches in hot beef broth for a savory and satisfying supper. Need another idea? Combine sliced beef with sauteed mushrooms, onions, some beef broth, and plenty of sour cream for beef stroganoff. Serve over noodles.

Red-Eye Chili keeps the family warm on cold winter nights, but how can you keep it new on the second go-round? Make Cincinnati-style chili by topping cooked spaghetti with hot chili Don't forget to heap on plenty of cheddar cheese! You can also use the reheated chili (and more cheese) to top hot dogs or fries. Or microwave the chili with several cups of cheddar cheese for a chili dip like no other!

Lighten Up

Savory slow-cooked meals can be as healthful as they are delicious. Substitute in reduced-fat dairy products like milk, sour cream, cream cheese, evaporated milk, cheeses, and margarine.

Gravy Separator

Lower-Sodium Products

Lower-fat products

Gravy Separator

Cut the fat from your sauces and gravies with the handy gravy separator. When the fat floats to the top, pour the liquid out.

Less Fat

To cut unneeded fat and calories from your slow-cooked foods, look for products that are labeled as reduced-fat, such as salad dressings, canned soups, marinara and Alfredo pasta sauces, and coconut milk.

Lower-Sodium Products

Slash sodium with ingredients like reduced-sodium black beans, soy sauce, broth, tomatoes, vegetables, and salt-free seasonings.

Supereasy Serve-Alongs

Turn your slow cooker dish into a meal by adding some quick and easy sides and desserts. Spruce up cakes and cookies from the bakery with sprinkles, coconut, fruit, ice cream, and more!

Vegetables

Add vegetables to the meal with bagged salad mix, canned vegetables, frozen vegetable mixes, or steam-in-the-bag vegetables (look in the produce section of your supermarket). Stir in butter and/or some of your favorite fresh herbs.

Deli Salads

Search the deli case at your supermarket for delicious salad options, such as coleslaw, baked beans, and pasta and potato salads. Customize these premade favorites by adding chopped fresh vegetables, herbs, or other ingredients.

Deli Salads

Vegetables

Side dishes

Breads

Side Dishes

Make it different every night by trying choices such as stuffing mixes, quick-cooking rice, refrigerated pastas, frozen french fries, or refrigerated mashed potatoes.

Bread

Soft on the inside, crusty on the outside—that's the best kind of bread! Cut thick slices from loaves or break rolls in half, then spread with plenty of butter. Another alternative is to flavor olive oil with herbs (such as basil, oregano, or thyme), add a little garlic, and dip pieces of bread in the mixture.

13

Slow Cooker Entertaining

For any occasion, big or small, the slow cooker deserves an invite. Keep this in mind: When you're busy prepping for a big dinner party, the oven is usually the star of the show. Make it easier by letting a side or dessert simmer in the slow cooker.

Tangy Pork Sandwiches

Sausage and Beer Beans

Thanksgiving in a Pot

Potlucks

Bring out the gingham table cloth and plastic forks—it's potluck time again! Bring one of these to your next gathering: Polynesian Pulled Pork (page 90), Tangy Pork Sandwiches (page 89), Marmalade BBQ Short Ribs (page 73), or a side like Baked Beans (page 48).

Tailgating

And now for tailgating season! It's time to cheer on your favorite sports team. Warm up the day with Red Eye Chili (page 56), Sausage and Beer Beans (page 52) (If desired, brown the sausages before adding to the slow cooker), or South-of-the-Border Beef Stew (page 139).

Holidays

Now you can join in the holiday fun with your friends and family—instead of being chained to the stove. Try your slow cooker at Thanksgiving with Thanksgiving in a Pot (page 27), Easter with Chicken Scaloppini with Spring Vegetables (page 23), or Christmas with Turkey with Green Chile Scalloped Potatoes (page 24).

Special Occasions

What about other occasions? For date night, try French Bistro Dinner (page 31). And dinner parties? Whip up Chicken with Vegetable Ragout and Polenta (page 32). For Sunday dinner, try Pot Roast Smothered with Bacon and Onions (page 40).

15

Warm-Up Drinks

Christmas Wassail

makes: 16 drinks

6 inches stick cinnamon, broken, *McCormick*®
12 whole cloves
6 cups water
1 12-ounce can frozen cranberry juice cocktail concentrate
1 12-ounce can frozen raspberry juice blend concentrate
1 12-ounce can frozen apple juice concentrate
1 cup brandy
⅓ cup lemon juice
¼ cup sugar

For a spice bag, cut a 6-inch square from a double thickness of 100-percent-cotton cheesecloth. Place cinnamon and cloves in center of square, bring up corners, and tie closed with a clean kitchen string. In a 4 to 6-quart slow cooker combine water, juice concentrates, brandy, lemon juice, and sugar. Add the spice bag to juice mixture. Cover; cook on low-heat setting for 4 to 6 hours or high-heat setting for 2 to 3 hours. Remove the spice bag and discard. Ladle into glasses.

Cranberry Punch Pizzazz

makes: 18 drinks

8 whole cardamom pods
16 inches stick cinnamon, broken, *McCormick*®
12 whole cloves
4 cups dry red wine, *Baron Philippe*® *Merlot*
1 11½- or 12-ounce can frozen cranberry juice concentrate
⅓ cup honey

Cut a 6-inch square from a double thickness of 100-percent-cotton cheesecloth for a spice bag. Pinch cardamom pods to break. Center the cadamom, cinnamon, and cloves on the cheesecloth square, bring up corners, and tie closed with clean kitchen string. In a 3½- to 6-quart slow cooker combine spice bag, wine, water, frozen juice concentrate, and honey. Cover; cook on low-heat setting for 4 to 6 hours or high-heat setting for 2 to 2½ hours. Remove and discard spice bag. Ladle into glasses.

Hot Spiced Sangria

makes: 12 drinks

2 bottles (750 ml each) Rioja (Spanish red wine)
2 bottles (750 ml each) white wine, *Sterling Vineyards*® *Sauvignon Blanc*
1 cup brandy
1 orange, sliced
2 cups frozen cherries, *Dole*®
2 cups frozen peaches, *Dole*®
2 cinnamon sticks, *McCormick*®
1 cup simple syrup

Combine all ingredients, except cinnamon stick garnish, in a 4½- to 5-quart slow cooker. Cover; cook on high-heat setting for 1 hour. Reduce to low-heat setting to hold temperature. Ladle into glasses. If desired, garnish with additional cinnamon sticks.

*Note: To make a simple syrup, combine 1 cup sugar with 1 cup water in a saucepan. Bring to a boil; reduce to a simmer. Stirring occasionally, simmer for 5 minutes or until sugar is dissolved.

Hot Apple Toddies

makes: 4 drinks

3 cups apple cider
4 cinnamon sticks, *McCormick*®
½ cup spiced rum, *Captain Morgan's*®
½ cup cinnamon schnapps, *Goldschlager*®
   Cinnamon sticks, for garnish, *McCormick*®

In a 4-quart slow cooker combine apple cider, 4 cinnamon sticks, spiced rum, and cinnamon schnapps. Cover; cook over high-heat setting for 1 hour. Ladle into glasses. Garnish with cinnamon sticks.

One-Pot Meals

One-pot meals claim a special place in my heart. Long before the slow cooker was even dreamed of, my grandma would set a big stew pot on the stove and start cleaning out the refrigerator. Leftover chicken parts became a savory broth, odds and ends vegetables became chunky filler, and a fistful of herbs made it all smell divine. She called it "kitchen sink stew," and while you never knew exactly what you were going to get, the laddering of flavor upon flavor made it all taste incredible.

It became a game—what could we add that would raise the taste to new levels? What serendipitous pairing of ingredients would create a new flavor combo? This chapter is filled with "keepers"—Pork Roast with Apples and Fennel, Corned Beef with Blackberry Mustard Sauce, Lamb Shanks with Pearl Barley and Root Vegetables. Just add a basket of bread for dunking, and you've got a nutritious full-meal menu.

The Recipes

Chicken with Fingerling Potatoes and Fennel

Prep 10 minutes
Cook Low 4 to 5 hours
Servings 4

1	pound assorted fingerling potatoes
3	fennel bulbs
4	boneless skinless chicken breasts, rinsed and patted dry
	Salt and pepper
1	can (10-ounce) condensed cream of celery soup, *Campbell's*®
¾	cup white wine, Chardonnay
1	teaspoon crushed garlic, *Christopher Ranch*®
1	tablespoon Fines Herbes, *Spice Islands*®

1. Place potatoes in a 5-quart slow cooker.

2. Remove tops from fennel bulbs and set aside. Cut fennel bulbs in half lengthwise, and slice into pieces, across the bulb. Place sliced fennel on top of potatoes.

3. Season chicken breasts with salt and pepper. Place in slow cooker on top of fennel.

4. Chop feathery parts of fennel tops, enough to equal 1 tablespoon. Place in a small bowl and add all remaining ingredients. Stir thoroughly and pour over chicken.

5. Cover and cook on LOW setting for 4 to 5 hours.

Asian-Style Steak Hot Pot

Prep 10 minutes
Cook Low 3 to 5 hours
Servings: 6

Slow cooking tenderizes tough cuts like flank steak, which otherwise tend to be a bit chewy. Szechwan spices add just enough heat to give you a little burn without upstaging the salty-sweet teriyaki-soy marinade.

- 1½ cups uncooked converted rice, *Uncle Ben's*®
- 3½ cups low-sodium beef stock, *Swanson*®
- 1½ pounds flank steak, rinsed and patted dry
- 1 packet (3/4-ounce) hot and spicy Szechwan mix, divided, *Sunbird*®
- 1 package (3.2-ounce) shiitake mushrooms, sliced
- 1½ cups frozen peas, *Birds Eye*®
- 2 scallions, sliced
- 1 tablespoon soy sauce, *Kikkoman*®
- 3 tablespoons teriyaki marinade, *Kikkoman*®

1. Combine rice and beef stock in a 5-quart slow cooker. Cut flank steak, against the grain, into thin strips. Season with one tablespoon of Szechwan mix. Place beef strips in slow cooker on top of rice.

2. In a medium bowl, combine sliced mushrooms, peas, and scallions; set aside. In a small bowl, whisk together soy sauce, teriyaki marinade, and remaining Szechwan mix. Pour over vegetables and toss thoroughly. Pour into the slow cooker over beef strips.

3. Cover and cook on LOW setting for 3 to 5 hours, or until rice is fully cooked.

Chicken Scaloppini with Spring Vegetables

Prep 10 minutes
Cook Low 4 hours
Servings 4

Dredging skinless chicken fillets in leek soup mix, instead of flour, gives them an earthy taste intensified by an asparagus soup broth. Cook meat and vegetables together, then serve them side by side for a pretty plate.

- 2½ cups seasoned diced potatoes, *Reser's*®
- 2 cups frozen sliced carrots, *Pictsweet*®
- 2 cups frozen early harvest peas, *C&W*®
- 2 cups frozen haricot verts, *C&W*®
  Salt and pepper
- 1 packet (1.8-ounce) leek soup mix, divided, *Knorr*®
- 2¼ pounds thin-sliced chicken breast fillets, rinsed and patted dry
- 1 can (10¾-ounce) condensed cream of asparagus soup, *Campbell's*®
- ½ cup white wine, Chardonnay

1. In a 5-quart slow cooker, combine all vegetables. In a small bowl, combine salt, pepper, and one tablespoon of leek soup mix. Dredge each fillet in the mixture, and place in slow cooker on top of vegetables.

2. In a medium bowl, whisk together asparagus soup, white wine, and remaining leek soup mix. Pour over chicken.

3. Cover and cook on LOW setting for 4 hours.

Turkey with Green Chile Scalloped Potatoes

Prep 10 minutes
Cook High 1 to 2 hours, **Low** 3½ to 4 hours
Servings 6

	Nonstick cooking spray
2	**pounds russet potatoes**
1	**package (8-ounce) 3-cheese crumbles, *Kraft*®**
¾	**cup cooked and crumbled bacon, *Hormel*®**
1	**can (4-ounce) diced green chiles, *Ortega*®**
1	**cup frozen chopped onions, *Ore-Ida*®**
2	**cans (10 ounce) condensed creamy chicken verde soup, divided, *Campbell's*®**
¼	**cup evaporated milk, *Carnation*®**
2	**pounds turkey breast cutlets, rinsed and patted dry**
	Salt and pepper

1. Spray inside of 5-quart slow cooker with cooking spray; set aside. Peel and slice potatoes ¼-inch thick. Soak in cold water until ready to use.

2. In a small bowl, combine cheese crumbles, bacon, diced chiles, and chopped onions. Layer potato slices and cheese mixture in the bottom of slow cooker.

3. In a small bowl, stir together one can of chicken verde soup with evaporated milk. Pour over potatoes and cheese. Cover and cook on HIGH setting for 1 to 2 hours.

4. Season turkey cutlets with salt and pepper, place on top of potatoes, and spread remaining can of soup over the top. Cover, switch to LOW setting, and cook for an additional 3½ to 4 hours.

Thanksgiving in a Pot

Prep 10 minutes
Cook Low 4 to 5 hours
Servings 6

1	box (6-ounce) cornbread stuffing mix, *Stove Top*®
1	cup low-sodium chicken broth, *Swanson*®
4	tablespoons butter
2	bags (8 ounces each) trimmed fresh haricots verts or French green beans, *Ready Pac*®
1	cup frozen pearl onions, *C&W*®
1	teaspoon kosher salt
1	teaspoon ground black pepper
1	teaspoon poultry seasoning, *McCormick*®
1	whole boneless skinless turkey breast, rinsed and patted dry
2	cans (15 ounces each) cut sweet potatoes, drained, *Princella*®
1	can (10-ounce) condensed cream of mushroom soup, *Campbell's*®
½	cup white wine, Chardonnay
1	packet (.95-ounce) turkey gravy mix, *Lawry's*®

1. Combine stuffing mix, chicken broth, and butter in a microwave-safe bowl. Cover and cook in microwave on HIGH for 5 minutes. Remove and set aside to cool.

2. Place green beans and onions in the bottom of a 5-quart slow cooker.

3. In a small bowl, mix together salt, pepper, and poultry seasoning. Season all sides of the turkey breast with mixture. Insert a pop-up thermometer in the thickest part of the breast. Place in the slow cooker, and surround the turkey breast with the sweet potatoes.

4. In a large bowl, stir together mushroom soup, white wine, and gravy mix. Pour over turkey and sweet potatoes. Spoon stuffing mixture around the turkey breast.

5. Cover and cook on LOW for 4 to 5 hours. Check to see that thermometer has popped up before serving.

Pork Roast with Apples and Fennel

Prep 10 minutes
Cook Low 6 hours
Servings 6

2	fennel bulbs
1	small onion, peeled and diced
2½	pounds boneless pork butt roast, rinsed and patted dry
1	teaspoon kosher salt
1	teaspoon ground black pepper
1	tablespoon Fines Herbes, *Spice Islands*®
1	bag (14-ounce) sliced green apples, *Chiquita*®
1	packet (1.8-ounce) white sauce mix, *Knorr*®
1	cup white wine, Chardonnay

1. Remove tops from fennel and slice the bulbs lengthwise. Combine fennel and onions in the bottom of a 5-quart slow cooker.

2. Season pork roast with salt, pepper, and Fines Herbes. Place in slow cooker on top of vegetables. Add the green apples.

3. In a small bowl, whisk together white sauce mix and white wine. Pour over pork roast.

4. Cover and cook on LOW setting for 6 hours.

Stewed Pork with Black-Eyed Peas

Prep 5 minutes
Cook Low 4 to 5 hours
Servings 6

2	pounds pork tenderloin, cut into bite-sized pieces
1	can (15-ounce) organic black-eyed peas, *Eden*®
2	cans (14½ ounces each) stewed tomatoes with onions, celery, and green peppers, *Del Monte*®
1	cup frozen chopped green peppers, *Pictsweet*®
1	cup uncooked converted rice, *Uncle Ben's*®
2	cups vegetable stock, *Kitchen Basics*®
1	tablespoon Cajun seasoning, *McCormick*®

1. In a 5-quart slow cooker, combine pork pieces, black-eyed peas, stewed tomatoes, and green peppers.

2. In a medium bowl, combine rice, vegetable stock, and Cajun seasoning. Pour into slow cooker and stir thoroughly.

3. Cover and cook on LOW setting for 4 to 5 hours.

French Country Bistro Dinner

Prep 8 minutes
Cook Low 4 to 6 hours
Servings 4

Herbes de Provence is a quick cook's delight, gathering the flavors of southern France in one blockbuster mix. Rosemary, thyme, lavender, tarragon, and a hint of mint make the sauce an irresistible backdrop to country vegetables and pork.

1	bag (14-ounce) frozen Parisienne carrots, *C&W®*
1	package (8-ounce) sliced fresh mushrooms
2	cups whole peeled tomatoes, *Muir Glen®*
1	can (15-ounce) cannellini beans, drained, *Progresso®*
4	boneless, thick-cut, pork loin chops, rinsed and patted dry
	Salt and pepper
1	tablespoon plus 1 teaspoon Herbes de Provence, divided
1	can (10¾-ounce) condensed cream of potato soup, *Campbell's®*
¼	cup Dijon mustard, *Grey Poupon®*
1	tablespoon tomato paste, *Contadina®*
3	tablespoons dry sherry, *Christian Brothers®*

1. In a 5-quart slow cooker, combine carrots, mushrooms, tomatoes, and beans.

2. Season pork chops with salt, pepper, and 1 tablespoon of Herbes de Provence. Place in slow cooker on top of vegetables.

3. In a small bowl, combine potato soup, Dijon mustard, tomato paste, sherry, and remaining teaspoon of Herbes de Provence. Pour over pork chops.

4. Cover and cook on LOW setting for 4 to 6 hours.

Chicken with Vegetable Ragout and Polenta

Prep 8 minutes
Cook Low 4 to 5 hours
Servings 6

3	cups frozen primavera vegetable medley, *Birds Eye®*
1	can (14-ounce) artichoke quarters in water, drained, *Maria®*
1	teaspoon garlic salt, *Lawry's®*
¾	teaspoon ground black pepper
1½	teaspoons Italian seasoning, *McCormick®*
6	chicken breasts, rinsed and patted dry
1	jar (14-ounce) pasta sauce, *Prego®*
¼	cup dry sherry, *Christian Brothers®*
1	teaspoon crushed garlic, *Christopher Ranch®*
3	tablespoons tomato paste, *Contadina®*
1	tube (24-ounce) pre-cooked polenta, sliced ½-inch thick, *Gennaro®*
	Grated parmesan cheese, for garnish

1. In a 5-quart slow cooker, combine frozen vegetable medley and artichokes.

2. In a small bowl, combine garlic salt, pepper, and Italian seasoning. Season both sides of the chicken breasts with mixture. Place chicken in slow cooker on top of vegetables.

3. In a large bowl, stir together pasta sauce, sherry, garlic, and tomato paste. Pour over chicken and vegetables. Top with polenta slices.

4. Cover and cook on LOW setting for 4 to 5 hours. Serve hot with grated parmesan cheese.

Corned Beef with Blackberry Mustard Sauce

Prep 10 minutes
Cook High 2 hours,
     Low 7 to 9 hours
Servings 6

2	medium sweet onions, peeled and cut into wedges
1	cup baby carrots
1	pound fingerling potatoes
3½	pounds corned beef brisket, rinsed and patted dry
2	teaspoons Montreal steak seasoning, *McCormick Grill Mates*®
1½	cups low-sodium beef broth, *Swanson*®
1	tablespoon salt-free seafood broil seasoning, *The Spice Hunter*®
2	tablespoons orange juice concentrate, *Minute Maid*®
¾	cup blackberry preserves, *Knott's Berry Farm*®
½	cup Dijon mustard, *Grey Poupon*®

1. In a 5-quart slow cooker, combine onions, carrots, and potatoes. Season corned beef with steak seasoning and place on top of vegetables, cutting to fit if necessary.

2. In a medium bowl, stir together beef broth, seafood seasoning, and orange juice concentrate. Pour over corned beef. Cover and cook on HIGH for 2 hours. Switch to LOW setting and cook for an additional 7 to 9 hours.

3. For blackberry mustard, combine blackberry preserves and Dijon mustard. Thin mustard with cooking liquid, if needed. Drizzle over corned beef.

Beef Roast with Cauliflower Puree

Prep 8 minutes
Cook Low 8 hours
Servings 6

2	pounds cauliflower flowerets, cleaned and trimmed
1	package (10-ounce) baby carrots
2	pounds beef chuck roast, rinsed and patted dry
2	teaspoons ground black pepper
1	envelope (1.1-ounce) beefy onion soup mix, divided, *Lipton*®
2	tablespoons garlic herb sauce mix, *Knorr*®
1	cup low-sodium beef broth, *Swanson*®
1	tablespoon butter
	Salt and pepper

1. In a 5-quart slow cooker, combine flowerets and carrots. Season beef roast with pepper and 1 tablespoon onion soup mix. Place on top of vegetables. In a small bowl, combine remaining onion soup mix, garlic herb mix, and beef broth. Pour over the beef roast and vegetables.

2. Cover and cook on LOW setting for 8 hours. Remove beef and carrots from the slow cooker. Transfer cauliflower with a slotted spoon to a blender or food processor. Add butter and puree until smooth. Season with salt and pepper to taste.

Caribbean Nights Dinner

Prep 10 minutes
Cook Low 6 hours
Servings 4

3	plantains, peeled and sliced ¼ inch thick
1	cup frozen seasoning blend, *Pictsweet*®
2	cans (15 ounces each) black beans, drained, *S&W*®
1½	pounds flank steak, rinsed and patted dry
	Salt and pepper
3	teaspoons salt-free Jamaican Jerk blend, divided, *The Spice Hunter*®
1	can (8-ounce) crushed pineapple in juice, *Dole*®
1	cup low-sodium beef broth, *Swanson*®

1. In a 5-quart slow cooker, combine plantains, seasoning blend, and beans.

2. Season flank steak with salt, pepper, and 1 teaspoon Jamaican Jerk blend. Place in slow cooker, cutting to fit if necessary.

3. In a medium bowl, combine crushed pineapple, beef broth, and remaining Jamaican jerk blend. Pour into the slow cooker over flank steak. Cover and cook on LOW setting for 6 hours.

4. Carefully remove flank steak and slice thinly across the grain. Serve hot with black beans and plantains.

St. Paddy's Day Dinner

Prep 10 minutes
Cook High 1 hour, **Low** 7 to 8 hours
Servings 6

1½	pounds baby white potatoes
1	teaspoon garlic powder, *McCormick®*
1	teaspoon red and black pepper blend, *McCormick®*
1	tablespoon seafood broil seasoning, *The Spice Hunter®* (optional)
3	pounds corned beef brisket, rinsed and patted dry, seasoning packet reserved
1	bottle (12-ounce) *Bass Ale®*
¼	cup plus 3 tablespoons apple cider vinegar, divided, *Heinz®*
¼	cup spicy brown mustard, *French's*
3	packages (8 ounces each) shredded red cabbage, *Ready Pac®*
1	teaspoon salt

1. Place potatoes in a 5-quart slow cooker.

2. In a small bowl, combine garlic powder and pepper blend. Add seasoning packet included with brisket. (If no packet is included, use 1 tablespoon of seafood broil seasoning.) Season both sides of the brisket with mixture. Place brisket on top of the potatoes, cutting to fit if necessary.

3. In a medium bowl, stir together Bass Ale, ¼ cup cider vinegar, and mustard. Pour into slow cooker over brisket. Cover and cook on HIGH setting for 1 hour. Switch to LOW setting and cook for 4 hours.

4. In a medium bowl, toss cabbage with remaining cider vinegar and salt. Add cabbage mixture to the slow cooker, pushing down on top of the brisket. Cover and cook on LOW setting for an additional 3 to 4 hours.

Serving Ideas: Accompany with two or three small pots of different deli mustards. Makes a great sandwich the day after!

Pot Roast Smothered with Bacon and Onions

Prep 8 minutes
Cook Low 8 to 10 hours
Servings 6

1	pound whole baby red skin potatoes, rinsed
3	pounds beef chuck roast, rinsed and patted dry
2	teaspoons Montreal Steak seasoning, *McCormick Grill Mates*®
1	box (1.9-ounce) pre-cooked bacon, *Eckrich Ready Crisp*®
1	can (10-ounce) condensed cream of mushroom soup, *Campbell's*®
1	packet (1.5-ounce) meatloaf seasoning, *McCormick*®
1	package (8-ounce) sliced fresh mushrooms
1	large onion, peeled and sliced

1. Place potatoes in the bottom of a 5-or 6-quart slow cooker.

2. Season both sides of the chuck roast with steak seasoning. Set on top of potatoes. Lay bacon slices over roast.

3. In a medium bowl, stir together soup and meatloaf seasoning. Pour over roast and bacon. Top with sliced mushrooms and onion. Cover and cook on LOW setting for 8 to 10 hours.

Steak and Potatoes with Bleu Cheese

Prep 10 minutes
Cook Low 8 hours
Servings 6

The English call it Stilton; the French, Roquefort; Italians, Gorgonzola. Whatever you call it, blue cheese is a taste powerhouse. Blended with bacon, garlic and onions in an assertive white sauce, it makes a cosmopolitan "beef and bleu."

2	pounds russet potatoes
½	cup frozen chopped onion, *Ore-Ida*®
1	container (4-ounce) crumbled bleu cheese, *Treasure Cave*®
¾	cup cooked and crumbled bacon, *Hormel*®
1	teaspoon crushed garlic, *Christopher Ranch*®
2	cans (10 ounces each) white sauce, divided, *Aunt Penny's*®
2	pounds bottom round steak, rinsed and patted dry
	Salt and pepper
2	tablespoons beef stew seasoning, *Lawry's*®

1. Peel and slice potatoes ¼-inch thick. Soak in cold water until ready to use.

2. In a large bowl, combine chopped onion, blue cheese, bacon, and garlic. Starting with potatoes, layer potatoes and blue cheese mixture in a 5-quart slow cooker. Pour one can of white sauce over mixture. Cut round steak into six portions and season each with salt and pepper. Place in slow cooker on top of potatoes and cheese.

3. In a medium bowl, stir together 1 can of white sauce with beef stew seasoning. Pour over steaks. Cover and cook on LOW setting for 8 hours.

Veal Roast with Bacon and Irish Whiskey Cream

Prep 10 minutes
Cook Low 6 to 7 hours
Servings 6

Irish whiskey cakes are among the moistest and richest you'll find. Steep bacon-wrapped veal, fingerling potatoes, and baby carrots in a similar whiskey-spiked potato sauce and it'll practically melt in your mouth.

1	pound fingerling potatoes
1½	cups baby carrots
3	celery ribs, chopped
3	pounds boneless veal shoulder roast, rinsed and patted dry
1	package (1.9-ounce) pre-cooked bacon, *Eckrich Ready Crisp*®
1	can (10¾-ounce) condensed cream of potato soup, *Campbell's*®
¼	cup Irish whiskey, *Jameson*®
1	teaspoon salt
1	teaspoon ground black pepper

1. In a 5-quart slow cooker, combine potatoes, carrots, and celery.

2. Cut veal roast into six individual portions. Wrap each with two to three slices of bacon. Place wrapped veal in slow cooker on top of vegetables.

3. In a medium bowl, stir together potato soup, Irish whiskey, salt, and pepper. Pour over roast and vegetables. Cover and cook on LOW setting for 6 to 7 hours.

Lamb Shanks with Pearl Barley and Root Vegetables

Prep 10 minutes
Cook Low 8 to 10 hours
Servings 4

½	cup pearl barley
1	cup frozen chopped onions, *Ore-Ida®*
2	parsnips, peeled and sliced
1	cup baby carrots, cut into 1/2-inch pieces
1	fennel bulb, chopped
4	lamb shanks, rinsed and patted dry
2	teaspoons Montreal steak seasoning, *McCormick Grill Mates®*
2	cups low-sodium beef broth, *Swanson®*
1	cup red wine, Cabernet Sauvignon
1	packet (0.9-ounce) onion and mushroom soup mix, *Lipton®*

1. In the bottom of a 5-quart slow cooker, combine barley, onions, parsnips, carrots, and fennel.

2. Season lamb shanks with steak seasoning and place in slow cooker on top of barley and vegetables.

3. In a medium bowl, stir together beef broth, red wine, and soup mix. Pour over lamb shanks.

4. Cover and cook on LOW setting for 8 to 10 hours.

Beans and Chili

I was in college in Wisconsin when I attended my first chili cookoff. And while all that sampling was four-alarm fun, I was amazed to realize that chili can be so much more than beef and beans. It can be ground turkey, lamb, chicken, or even tofu, enlivened with an array of exotic ingredients, from mild-mannered mango to red-hot chile peppers.

This chapter is a chili lover's paradise, with unusual entrées that take their flavor from the unlikeliest of ingredients—instant coffee, tropical fruits, pumpkin pie spice. Stir in molasses and cloves to give baked beans a boost of flavor. Add a wiener and bun and Chili Colorado becomes a Wild West chili dog. Wrap California Black Bean Chili in a warm tortilla, and you have a turkey burrito. Or mix any chili with macaroni to make kid-friendly Chili-Mac. It's a delicious way to lure taste buds to a high-fiber food that's fabulous.

The Recipes

Baked Beans

Prep 8 minutes
Cook High 4 to 6 hours
Servings 12

5	cans (15 ounces each) navy beans, drained, *Great Northern*®
1	small onion, peeled and diced
¾	cup cooked, crumbled bacon, *Hormel*®
¾	cup molasses, *Grandma's*®
1	cup ketchup, *Heinz*®
¼	cup yellow mustard, *French's*®
½	teaspoon pumpkin pie spice, *McCormick*®
½	teaspoon ground cloves
	Salt and pepper

1. In a 4-quart slow cooker, combine beans, onion, and crumbled bacon.

2. In a medium bowl, stir together molasses, ketchup, mustard, pumpkin pie spice, and cloves. Pour into slow cooker and stir thoroughly.

3. Cover and cook on HIGH setting for 4 to 6 hours.

4. Season with salt and pepper to taste.

Cajun Red Beans with Andouille Sausage

Prep 8 minutes
Cook High 3 to 4 hours
Servings 6

Two New Orleans favorites—red beans and rice and spicy andouille sausage—come together in this gumbo-style stew. It's definitely the Big Easy—just add a can of Mexican tomatoes, green peppers, rice, and seasonings and let it simmer all day.

1	package (13-ounce) Cajun style andouille sausage, diced, *Aidells®*
2	cans (15 ounces each) kidney beans, drained, *S&W®*
1	can (14.5-ounce) diced tomatoes with onions and green peppers, *S&W®*
½	cup frozen chopped green peppers, *Pictsweet®*
¾	cup converted rice, *Uncle Ben's®*
2	cups vegetable stock, *Kitchen Basics®*
1	tablespoon Cajun seasoning, *McCormick®*
	Salt and pepper

1. In a 4-quart slow cooker, combine sausage, beans, tomatoes, and green peppers.

2. In a medium bowl, stir together rice, vegetable stock, and Cajun seasoning. Pour into slow cooker and stir thoroughly.

3. Cover and cook on HIGH setting for 3 to 4 hours. Season with salt and pepper to taste.

Sausage and Beer Beans

Prep 10 minutes
Cook High 4 to 5 hours
Servings 6

Beans and bratwurst is Wisconsin's soul food, so if you haven't had it, you're in for a tailgate treat! If you're already a fan, you'll applaud it this way, simmered in cheddar cheese and Dijon, with dark ale to deepen the flavor.

3	cans (16 ounces each) pinto beans, drained, *Bush's*®
1	cup diced tomatoes, drained, *Muir Glen*®
½	cup frozen seasoning blend, *Pictsweet*®
6	bratwurst sausages, scored
2	tablespoons Dijon mustard, *Grey Poupon*®
1	can (10 3/4-ounce) condensed cheddar cheese soup, *Campbell's*®
1	teaspoon crushed garlic, *Christopher Ranch*®
½	cup *Bass Ale*® (or any dark ale)

1. In a 4-quart slow cooker, combine beans, tomatoes, and seasoning blend. Top with scored sausages.

2. In a medium bowl, stir together mustard, cheese soup, garlic, and Bass Ale until smooth. Pour into slow cooker and stir thoroughly.

3. Cover and cook on HIGH setting for 4 to 5 hours.

Caribbean Beans and Rice

Prep 5 minutes
Cook High 4 to 5 hours
Servings 6

3	cans (10 ounces each) Caribbean recipe beans, *S&W*®
1	cup converted rice, uncooked, *Uncle Ben's*®
1	cup frozen chopped green peppers, *Pictsweet*®
1	cup frozen chopped onions, *Ore-Ida*®
½	tablespoon crushed garlic, *Christopher Ranch*®
2	tablespoons tomato paste, *Contadina*®
2	tablespoons salt-free Jamaican Jerk blend, *The Spice Hunter*®
1½	cups low-sodium chicken broth, *Swanson*®

1. In a 4-quart slow cooker, combine beans, rice, green peppers, and onions.

2. In a medium bowl, whisk together garlic, tomato paste, Jamaican Jerk blend, and chicken broth. Pour into slow cooker and stir thoroughly.

3. Cover and cook on HIGH setting for 4 to 5 hours.

Red-Eye Chili

Prep 5 minutes
Cook High 4 to 6 hours
Servings 8

This Texas-style chili takes its name from the surprise ingredient—coffee—which gives Red-Eye Gravy its perky taste. My version sweetens the coffee with brown sugar and adds green chile tomatoes to enliven the lighter-than-beef pork shoulder.

2	pounds pork shoulder or pork stew meat, cut into bite-sized pieces
	Salt and pepper
2	cans (15 ounces each) kidney beans, drained, *S&W*®
2	cans (14 ounces each) diced tomatoes with green chiles, drained, *Muir Glen*®
1	cup frozen chopped onions, *Ore-Ida*®
2	packets (1.25 ounces each) mild chili seasoning, *McCormick*®
2	tablespoons instant coffee granules, *Folgers*®
2	tablespoons light brown sugar

1. Season pork with salt and pepper and place in a 4-quart slow cooker.

2. Add remaining ingredients and stir thoroughly to combine.

3. Cover and cook on HIGH setting for 4 to 6 hours.

Chili Colorado

Prep 8 minutes
Cook High 4 to 6 hours
Servings 6

2	pounds beef stew meat, cut into bite-sized pieces
	Salt and pepper
1	small red onion, peeled and finely diced
3	cans (4 ounces each) diced green chiles, *Ortega*®
¼	cup cooked and crumbled bacon, *Hormel*®
1	cup tomato puree, *Progresso*®
1	tablespoon salt-free Mexican seasoning, *The Spice Hunter*®
½	teaspoon chili powder, *Gebhardt's*®
½	cup low-sodium beef broth, *Swanson*®

1. Season stew meat with salt and pepper and place in a 4-quart slow cooker. Add onion, green chiles, and bacon.

2. In a small bowl, whisk together tomato puree, Mexican seasoning, chili powder, and beef broth. Pour into slow cooker and stir thoroughly.

3. Cover and cook on HIGH setting for 4 to 6 hours.

California Black Bean Chili

Prep 10 minutes
Cook High 4 to 6 hours
Servings 6

1¼	pounds ground turkey
	Salt and pepper
2	cans (15 ounces each) black beans, drained, *S&W*®
1	can (7-ounce) diced green chiles, *Ortega*®
1	can (14-ounce) diced fire-roasted tomatoes, *Muir Glen*®
1	can (8-ounce) tomato sauce, *Hunt's*®
3	cups diced zucchini
1	cup frozen chopped onions, *Ore-Ida*®
1	packet (1.5-ounce) chili seasoning mix, *McCormick*®
1	tablespoon chili power, *Gebhardt's*®
1	teaspoon crushed garlic, *Christopher Ranch*®
	Diced avocado or guacamole, for garnish

1. In a large skillet, brown ground turkey, stirring frequently. Season with salt and pepper. Drain and transfer to a 4-quart slow cooker.

2. Add remaining ingredients, except avocado, to slow cooker. Stir thoroughly.

3. Cover and cook on HIGH setting for 4 to 6 hours.

4. Serve hot with avocado garnish.

Mango Chili

Prep 5 minutes
Cook High 4 to 6 hours
Servings 6

Chunks of mango stand in for meat in a vegetarian four-bean chili that's an intriguing dance between sweet and spicy. Mango nectar and rum provide the sweet, while Mexican tomatoes, chili seasonings, and a dash of curry add heat.

1	can (15-ounce) pinto beans, drained, *Bush's*®
1	can (15-ounce) black beans, drained, *S&W*®
1	can (15-ounce) kidney beans, drained, *S&W*®
1	can (15-ounce) cannellini beans, drained, *Progresso*®
2	cups frozen mango chunks, *Dole*®
2	cans (10 ounces each) Mexican diced tomatoes, *Ro-Tel*®
1	packet (1.5-ounce) chili seasoning mix, *McCormick*®
1	tablespoon curry powder, *McCormick*®
3	tablespoons tomato paste, *Contadina*®
½	cup mango nectar, *Kern's*®
½	cup mango rum, *Malibu*®
	Sour cream, for garnish
	Fresh cilantro, chopped, for garnish

1. Combine all ingredients, except sour cream and cilantro, in a 4-quart slow cooker. Stir thoroughly.

2. Cover and cook on HIGH setting for 4 to 6 hours.

3. Serve hot, topped with sour cream and cilantro garnish.

Beefy Beany Bourbon Chili

Prep 10 minutes
Cook High 4 to 6 hours
Servings 6

1	pound lean ground beef
	Salt and pepper
1	pound beef stew meat, cut into bite-sized pieces
3	cans (15 ounces each) pinto beans, drained, *Bush's*®
1	can (4-ounce) diced green chiles, *Ortega*®
1	packet (1.1-ounce) beefy onion soup mix, *Lipton*®
2	packets (1.25 ounces each) chili seasoning mix, *McCormick*®
1	bottle (12-ounce) chili sauce, *Heinz*®
¾	cup bourbon, *Jim Beam*®

1. In a large skillet, brown ground beef, stirring frequently. Season with salt and pepper. Drain and transfer to a 4-quart slow cooker.

2. Add all remaining ingredients and stir thoroughly.

3. Cover and cook on HIGH setting for 4 to 6 hours.

Sweet and Sassy Chili with Corn Bread Crust

Prep 10 minutes
Cook High 5 hours
Servings 6

1	pound ground pork
1	pound ground beef
2	packets (1.25 ounces each) chipotle seasoning mix, divided, *Ortega*®
3	cans (15.25 ounces each) low-sodium kidney beans, drained, *S&W*®
½	cup cooked and crumbled bacon, *Hormel*®
2	cans (28 ounces each) diced tomatoes, *Ro-tel*®
1	teaspoon pumpkin pie spice, *McCormick*®
1½	cups tomato sauce, *Contadina*®
¼	cup tomato paste, *Contadina*®
¼	cup honey, *Sue Bee*®
1	box (8.5-ounce) corn muffin mix, *Jiffy*®
1	large egg
⅓	cup milk

1. In a large skillet, brown ground pork and ground beef together with one packet chipotle seasoning. Drain and transfer to a 5-quart slow cooker. Add beans and bacon and stir thoroughly.

2. In a large bowl, combine diced tomatoes, remaining packet chipotle seasoning, pumpkin pie spice, tomato sauce, tomato paste, and honey. Pour into slow cooker and stir thoroughly.

3. Cover and cook on HIGH setting for 3½ to 4 hours.

4. In a medium bowl, combine muffin mix, egg, and milk. Stir until well combined (mixture will be slightly lumpy). Remove slow cooker lid and pour mixture over the top of the chili. Place 6 paper towels on top of the slow cooker and secure with lid. (This helps to trap steam.)

5. Cover and cook on HIGH setting for an additional 1 hour.

Serving ideas: Serve hot with extra honey and butter for corn bread.

5-Ingredient Dishes

Whether we work out of the home or in it, every year seems busier than the last. These days, if I can cross five items off my to-do list, it's a major accomplishment. Five items is doable, whether you're planning a project… or a meal. Start with a canned soup stock, layer in vegetables, fruits, meat, and seasonings, then stir and simmer into a dish that's greater than the sum of its parts.

Every recipe in this chapter is a delicious reminder that less is more. The trick is to use big-flavor ingredients, imaginatively combined to create an intricate depth of taste. Chicken breasts come alive with red onions and salsa. Dates and bacon give turkey texture and zest. Pistachios, honey, and cinnamon turn humble pork chops into a fancy feast. Forget a laundry list of ingredients. Say goodbye to hours in the kitchen. Toss a handful of ingredients into a pot and cross dinner off your list.

The Recipes

Beef and Mushroom Hot Pot

Prep 5 minutes
Cook Low 6 to 8 hours
Servings 6

2	pounds beef stew meat, cut into bite-sized pieces
	Salt and pepper
2	packages (8 ounces each) sliced fresh mushrooms
2	cups frozen sliced carrots, *Birds Eye*®
1	box (6-ounces) long-grain and wild rice blend, *Uncle Ben's*®
2	cans (14 ounces each) low-sodium beef broth, *Swanson*®

1. Season stew meat with salt and pepper and place in a 5-quart slow cooker. Add all remaining ingredients and stir thoroughly.

2. Cover and cook on LOW setting for 6 to 8 hours.

Marmalade BBQ Short Ribs

Prep 8 minutes
Cook Low 8 to 10 hours
Servings 4

When it comes to real down-home BBQ, Texans say the stickier the better. These ribs pass muster, getting their unique, sugary flavor and texture from orange marmalade mixed with BBQ sauce. Pair it with pork or beef and a big pile of napkins.

 2 small onions, peeled and sliced
 12 beef short ribs, rinsed and patted dry
 Salt and pepper
 ½ cup marmalade, *Knott's Berry Farm®*
 ¾ cup sweet & sticky BBQ rib sauce, *Bull's-Eye®*
 1 envelope (1-ounce) onion soup mix, *Lipton®*

1. Place onions in the bottom of a 5-quart slow cooker. Season short ribs with salt and pepper and place in slow cooker on top of onions.

2. In a small bowl, stir together all remaining ingredients. Pour over short ribs. Cover and cook on LOW setting for 8 to 10 hours.

3. Remove ribs from slow cooker, and strain and defat the cooking liquid. Serve warm, as sauce, on the side.

Drambuie Beef

Prep 10 minutes
Cook Low 8 to 10 hours
Servings 4

Red wine is the quintessential marinade for beef. Drambuie adds an intriguing topnote of herbed honey. Combining the two produces a vibrant, velvety smooth sauce that's just right for the holidays or special occasions.

 ½ medium onion, peeled and sliced
 1 cup *Drambuie®**
 ½ cup red wine, Merlot
 1 packet (1.5-ounce) beef stew seasoning, *Lawry's®*
 2 pounds round steak, rinsed and patted dry
 Salt and pepper
 1 tablespoon Herbes de Provence

1. Place onions in bottom of a 4-quart slow cooker. In a medium bowl, whisk together Drambuie, red wine, and beef stew seasoning. Set aside.

2. Cut round steak into serving portions and season each with salt, pepper, and Herbes de Provence. Place in slow cooker and pour Drambuie mixture over round steaks.

3. Cover and cook on LOW setting for 8 to 10 hours.

*Drambuie is a Scotch-based liqueur found at most grocery stores and liquor stores.

Creole Brisket

Prep 10 minutes
Cook Low 8 to 10 hours
Servings 6

1	package (4 count) mixed bell peppers, sliced, *Ready Pac*®
3	pounds brisket, rinsed and patted dry
	Salt and pepper
2	cans (14.5 ounces each) diced tomatoes with green peppers, celery, and onion, *Hunt's*®
1	tablespoon Creole seasoning, *McCormick*®
¼	cup Pernod

1. Place peppers in the bottom of a 5-quart slow cooker.

2. Season brisket with salt and pepper. Place in slow cooker on top of peppers. In a medium bowl, combine tomatoes, Creole seasoning, and Pernod. Pour over brisket.

3. Cover and cook on LOW setting for 8 to 10 hours. Let meat rest for 5 to 10 minutes before slicing.

Szechwan Beef

Prep 10 minutes
Cook Low 5 to 6 hours
Servings 4

3	red bell peppers, cut into 1-inch pieces
1	large sweet onion, peeled and cut into 1-inch pieces
2	pounds flank steak, rinsed and patted dry
2	tablespoons Szechwan seasoning, *McCormick*®
1	bottle (12.1-ounce) stir-fry sauce, *Kikkoman*®

1. In a 5-quart slow cooker, combine pepper and onions

2. Season both sides of the flank steak with Szechwan seasoning. Roll up steak starting from the narrowest end. Secure with butcher's twine. Place in slow cooker on top of vegetables. Pour stir-fry sauce over flank steak.

3. Cover and cook on LOW setting for 5 to 6 hours.

4. Remove flank steak from the slow cooker and let rest for 5 to 10 minutes before slicing. Slice across the rolled steak to serve.

Short Ribs Provençale

Prep 10 minutes
Cook Low 8 to 10 hours
Servings 6

1	large onion, peeled and thickly sliced
12	beef short ribs, rinsed and patted dry
	Salt and pepper
2	tablespoons Herbes de Provence
1	cup French dressing deluxe, *Wish-Bone*®
1	can (10½-ounce) condensed French onion soup, *Campbell's*®

1. Place onions in the bottom of a 5-quart slow cooker.

2. Season short ribs with salt, pepper, and Herbes de Provence. Place short ribs, meat side up, in slow cooker.

3. In a small bowl, whisk together French dressing and French onion soup. Pour over short ribs.

4. Cover and cook on LOW setting for 8 to 10 hours.

Chicken with Red Onion Salsa

Prep 5 minutes
Cook Low 4 to 6 hours
Servings 4

4	chicken breast halves, rinsed and patted dry
2	tablespoons Mexican seasoning, *McCormick®*
2	cans (10 ounces each) Mexican diced tomatoes, *Ro-Tel®*
1	can (6-ounce) tomato paste, *Contadina®*
2	medium red onions, peeled and finely diced

1. Season both sides of chicken breasts with Mexican seasoning and set aside.

2. In a medium bowl, stir together diced tomatoes, tomato paste, and onions.

3. Pour half of salsa mixture in the bottom of a 5-quart slow cooker. Add chicken and top with remaining salsa mixture.

4. Cover and cook on LOW setting for 4 to 6 hours.

Sunset Chicken

Prep 5 minutes
Cook Low 3 to 4 hours
Servings 4

Tangy Catalina dressing and orange juice give this mood-boosting main course the sunny flavors of warmer climes. The sauce shimmers in shades from amber to crimson, so let it puddle on the plate for a glorious effect.

1	package (4 count) mixed bell peppers, cut into thick strips, *Ready Pac*®
2	pounds chicken breast tenders, rinsed and patted dry
	Salt and pepper
2	tablespoons salt-free citrus herb seasoning, *Spice Islands*®
1	cup Catalina dressing, *Kraft*®
2	tablespoons frozen orange juice concentrate, thawed, *Minute Maid*®

1. Place bell peppers in the bottom of a 5-quart slow cooker.

2. Season both sides of chicken tenders with salt, pepper, and citrus herb seasoning. Place in slow cooker on top of bell peppers.

3. In a small bowl, stir together Catalina dressing and orange juice concentrate. Pour in slow cooker over chicken.

4. Cover and cook on LOW setting for 3 to 4 hours.

Miso Chicken with Mushrooms

Prep 5 minutes
Cook Low 3 to 4 hours
Servings 4

2	packages (8 ounces each) sliced fresh brown mushrooms
4	scallions, cut into 1-inch pieces, plus extra for garnish
4	boneless skinless chicken breasts, rinsed and patted dry
1	package (1.5-ounce, 3 individual packets) tofu miso soup mix, *Kikkoman*®
1	cup sake

1. Combine mushrooms and scallions in the bottom of a 5-quart slow cooker. Place chicken breasts on top of mushrooms and scallions.

2. In a small bowl, dissolve tofu miso soup mix in 2 cups of warm water. Stir in the sake and pour over chicken.

3. Cover and cook on LOW setting for 3 to 4 hours.

Serving ideas: Serve hot with scallion garnish.

Borracho Chicken

Prep 5 minutes
Cook Low 3 to 4 hours
Servings 4

2   cans (16 ounces each) pinto beans, undrained, *Bush's®*
4   boneless skinless chicken breasts, rinsed and patted dry
      Salt and pepper
2   cans (10 ounces each) Mexican diced tomatoes, *Ro-Tel®*
¼   cup gold tequila, *Jose Cuervo®*
1   tablespoon salt-free fajita seasoning, *The Spice Hunter®*

1. Place pinto beans in the bottom of a 5-quart slow cooker.

2. Season chicken breasts with salt and pepper. Place in slow cooker on top of pinto beans.

3. In a medium bowl, stir together diced tomatoes, tequila, and fajita seasoning. Pour over chicken.

4. Cover and cook on LOW setting for 3 to 4 hours.

Green Curry Chicken

Prep 5 minutes
Cook Low 3 to 4 hours
Servings 4

2	pounds chicken tenders, rinsed and patted dry
	Salt and pepper
1	can (8-ounce) sliced bamboo shoots, *La Choy*®
1	can (15-ounce) whole peeled straw mushrooms, *Dynasty*®
1½	tablespoons green curry paste, *Thai Kitchen*®
1	can (14-ounce) organic coconut milk, *Thai Kitchen*®
	Fresh cilantro, chopped, to garnish

1. Season chicken tenders with salt and pepper and place in the bottom of a 5-quart slow cooker. Add bamboo shoots and straw mushrooms.

2. In a medium bowl, whisk together curry paste and coconut milk. Pour in slow cooker and stir to combine.

3. Cover and cook on LOW setting for 3 to 4 hours.

Serving ideas: Serve hot with cilantro garnish.

Turkey Oreganata

Prep 5 minutes
Cook Low 3 to 4 hours
Servings 4

Peppery oregano, garlic, and onions in an Italian-style tomato sauce lend a pizzeria taste to turkey cutlets. Ladle it over pasta noodles or serve it in a deli roll for a healthful variation on meatball subs.

2 cans (14.5 ounces each) diced tomatoes with garlic, oregano, and basil, *S&W®*
1 can (6-ounce) tomato paste with Italian herbs, *Contadina®*
2 teaspoons oregano, *McCormick®*
1½ pounds turkey cutlets, rinsed and patted dry
   Salt and pepper
1 large onion, peeled and sliced thin

1. In a medium bowl, stir together diced tomatoes, tomato paste, and oregano and set aside. Season cutlets with salt and pepper and set aside.

2. Place half of the sliced onion in the bottom of a 5-quart slow cooker. Add half the turkey cutlets. Top with half of the tomato mixture, and repeat layers.

3. Cover and cook on LOW setting for 3 to 4 hours.

Turkey with Dates and Bacon

Prep 5 minutes
Cook Low 3½ to 4½ hours
Servings 4

1 medium sweet onion, peeled and sliced
1 pound boneless skinless turkey breast, rinsed and patted dry
   Salt and pepper
1 can (10¾-ounce) condensed cream of potato soup, *Campbell's®*
½ cup cooked and crumbled bacon, *Hormel®*
1 cup pitted dates, *Sunsweet®*

1. Place onions in the bottom of a 5-quart slow cooker.

2. Season turkey breast with salt and pepper. Insert a pop-up thermometer in the thickest part of the breast. Place in slow cooker on top of onions.

3. Pour potato soup over turkey. Top with bacon and dates.

4. Cover and cook on LOW setting for 3½ to 4½ hours. (Check to see that thermometer has popped up before serving.)

Tangy Pork Sandwiches

Prep 5 minutes
Cook Low 8 to 9 hours
Servings 8

1	large sweet onion, peeled and sliced
3	pounds boneless pork butt, rinsed and patted dry
	Salt and pepper
1	cup Catalina salad dressing, *Kraft®*
½	cup yellow mustard, *French's®*
3	tablespoons tomato paste, *Contadina®*
	White hamburger buns

1. Place onion in the bottom of a 5-quart slow cooker.

2. Season pork butt with salt and pepper. Place in slow cooker on top of onions, fat side up.

3. In a medium bowl, stir together Catalina dressing, mustard, and tomato paste. Pour over pork.

4. Cover and cook on LOW setting for 8 to 9 hours.

5. Remove pork and let rest for 5 to 10 minutes before slicing.

Serving ideas: Serve sliced pork on buns with sauce.

Polynesian Pulled Pork

Prep 8 minutes
Cook Low 8 to 9 hours
Servings 8

4	red bell peppers, cut into ½-inch strips
3	pounds boneless pork shoulder roast, rinsed and patted dry
	Salt and pepper
1	bottle (10-ounce) sweet & tangy sauce, *San-J*®
1	can (8-ounce) crushed pineapple, *Dole*®
½	cup chili sauce, *Heinz*®
	Hawaiian sweet buns for serving, *King's*®

1. Place peppers in the bottom of a 5-quart slow cooker.

2. Season pork with salt and pepper. Place in slow cooker, on top of peppers, fat side up.

3. In a medium bowl, stir together sweet & tangy sauce, pineapple, and chili sauce. Pour over pork roast. Cover and cook on LOW setting for 8 to 9 hours.

4. Remove pork and let rest for 5 to 10 minutes. Strain and defat cooking liquid. When cool enough to handle, pull or chop pork.

Serving ideas: Serve with peppers and sauce on the sweet buns.

Pork Chops in Tarragon Cream Sauce

Prep 8 minutes
Cook Low 4 to 5 hours
Servings: 4

1	bag (14-ounce) frozen pear onions, *C&W*®
4	boneless, thick-cut pork loin chops, rinsed and patted dry
	Salt and pepper
3	teaspoons dried tarragon, divided
1	can (10.5-ounce) white sauce, *Aunt Penny's*®
½	cup white wine, Chardonnay

1. Place pearl onions in the bottom of a 5-quart slow cooker.

2. Season pork chops with salt, pepper, and1 teaspoon dried tarragon. Place pork chops in slow cooker on top of pearl onions.

3. In a medium bowl, stir together white sauce, white wine, and remaining teaspoons dried tarragon. Pour over pork chops. Cover and cook on LOW setting for 4 to 5 hours.

Maple Jack Pork Chops

Prep 5 minutes
Cook Low 4 to 5 hours
Servings 4

Opposites definitely attract. Robust Dijon mustard and mellow maple syrup come together in a caramelized glaze that makes meaty pork loin chops a cut above. Sweet onions and a tipple of Jack Daniels add an unexpected twang.

1	large sweet onion, peeled and sliced
4	boneless, thick-cut pork loin chops, rinsed and patted dry
	Salt and pepper
½	cup pure Grade A maple syrup, *Spring Tree*®
¼	cup whiskey, *Jack Daniels*®
2	tablespoons Dijon mustard, *Grey Poupon*®

1. Place onions in the bottom of a 4-or 5-quart slow cooker.

2. Season pork chops with salt and pepper. In a small bowl, whisk together maple syrup, whiskey, and Dijon mustard. Dip each pork chop into the syrup mixture and place in slow cooker on top of onions. Pour remaining syrup mixture over pork chops.

3. Cover and cook on LOW setting for 4 to 5 hours.

Honey-Cinnamon Pork Chops with Carrots

Prep 5 minutes
Cook Low 4 to 5 hours
Servings 4

1	bag (16-ounce) frozen sliced carrots, *Birds Eye*®
4	boneless, thick-cut pork loin chops, rinsed and patted dry
	Salt and pepper
1	can (10¾-ounce) condensed tomato soup, *Campbell's*®
1	tablespoon ground cinnamon, *McCormick*®
⅓	cup honey, *Sue Bee*®
2	tablespoons unsalted, shelled pistachios, chopped, for garnish (optional)
¼	cup golden raisins, for garnish, *Sun-Maid*® (optional)

1. Place carrots in the bottom of a 5-quart slow cooker.

2. Season pork chops with salt and pepper. Place in slow cooker on top of the carrots.

3. In a small bowl, stir together tomato soup, cinnamon, and honey. Pour over pork chops. Cover and cook on LOW setting for 4 to 5 hours.

Serving ideas: Serve hot, topped with pistachio and golden raisin garnishes.

Poultry

It's inexpensive. It's easy. And it's healthy, too. Poultry is one of the best sources of low-fat protein, yet its greatest virtue just may be that there's something for everyone. Drumsticks, thighs, wings, breasts—even the giblets and gravy—one entrée satisfies a whole family of appetites. Growing up, my sisters and brothers and I all liked something different, so we'd rush to the table to stake our claim. A generation later, my nieces and nephews do the same.

This chapter serves up all sorts of poultry with all sorts of sauces. Juicy dark meat thighs have a heartiness balanced by thicker sauces, like a West Indies peanut satay. Milder white meat breasts come into their own with a lighter, sweeter orange-bourbon sauce. And while homey Chicken Paprika is just right for family night, Turkey with Saffron Nut Sauce makes a pretty date plate. Serve it with a side of well-dressed greens for an impress-anyone meal.

The Recipes

Chicken with Cumin-Date Sauce

Prep 10 minutes
Cook Low 3½–4½ hours
Servings 4

1	can (14-ounce) low-sodium chicken broth, *Swanson®*
½	cup red wine, Pinot Noir
2	tablespoons lemon juice, *ReaLemon®*
1	tablespoon ground cumin, *McCormick®*
1	teaspoon paprika, *McCormick®*
4	boneless skinless chicken breasts, rinsed and patted dry
	Salt and pepper
1	teaspoon Fines Herbes, *Spice Islands®*
6	garlic cloves, whole, *Christopher Ranch®*
1	cup pitted dates, *Sunsweet®*
2	tablespoons cold butter, cut into 4 chunks

1. In a small bowl, whisk together chicken broth, red wine, lemon juice, cumin, and paprika. Pour half of the liquid into the bottom of a 5-quart slow cooker.

2. Season chicken with salt, pepper, and Fines Herbes. Place in slow cooker and add whole garlic cloves. Pour remaining liquid over the chicken and top with dates.

3. Cover and cook on LOW setting for 3½ to 4½ hours.

4. Remove chicken from slow cooker and keep warm. Pour sauce, dates, and garlic through a fine mesh strainer into a medium saucepan, using the back of a wooden spoon to push as much of the essence of the cooked garlic and dates into the sauce as possible.

5. Bring the sauce to a boil and reduce by half. Lower temperature to a simmer and whisk in chunks of cold butter one at a time.

West Indies Chicken

Prep 10 minutes
Cook Low 3½ to 4½ hours
Servings 6

6	boneless skinless chicken thighs, rinsed and patted dry
2	cans (15 ounces each) chickpeas, drained, *Progresso*®
1	cup frozen chopped onions, *Ore-Ida*®
1	cup frozen chopped green peppers, *Pictsweet*®
⅓	cup golden raisins, *Sun-Maid*®
1	jar (8-ounce) peanut satay sauce, *Thai Kitchen*®
1	can (14-ounce) low-sodium chicken broth, *Swanson*®
½	teaspoon red pepper flakes, *McCormick*®
1½	teaspoons crushed garlic, *Christopher Ranch*®
1	can (15-ounce) cut sweet potatoes, drained and diced, *Princella*®

1. Trim excess fat from chicken thighs and cut into bite-sized pieces. Place in a 4-quart slow cooker. Add chickpeas, onions, green peppers, and raisins.

2. In a large bowl, stir together satay sauce, chicken broth, red pepper flakes, and garlic. Pour into slow cooker and stir thoroughly.

3. Cover and cook on HIGH setting for 3½ to 4½ hours. Stir in sweet potatoes. Cover and cook on LOW setting for an additional 1 hour.

Serving Ideas: Serve over steamed white rice with toasted sesame seeds.

Cheddar-Beer Chicken

Prep 5 minutes
Cook Low 3½ to 4½ hours
Servings 4

1	large onion, peeled and diced large
1	package (16-ounce) diced red potatoes, *Reser's®*
1	cup frozen diced green pepper, *Pictsweet®*
4	boneless skinless chicken breasts, rinsed and patted dry
1½	teaspoons garlic salt, *McCormick®*
1½	teaspoons ground black pepper
1	can (10-ounce) condensed cheddar cheese soup, *Campbell's®*
¾	cup *Bass Ale®*
¾	cup bacon crumbles, *Hormel®*
	Fresh chives, finely chopped, for garnish

1. In a 5-quart slow cooker, combine onion, potatoes, and green peppers.

2. Season both sides of chicken breasts with garlic salt and pepper. Place in slow cooker on top of vegetables.

3. In a small bowl, stir together cheddar soup, Bass Ale, and bacon crumbles. Pour over chicken.

4. Cover and cook on LOW setting for 3½ to 4½ hours.

Serving ideas: Serve hot with chive garnish.

Chicken Paprika

Prep 8 minutes
Cook Low 3½ to 4½ hours
Servings 6

1	large onion, peeled and quartered
1	package (8-ounce) sliced fresh mushrooms
2	pounds boneless skinless chicken thighs, rinsed and patted dry
	Salt and pepper
1⅓	tablespoons Hungarian paprika, divided
1	can (10¾-ounce) condensed cream of mushroom with roasted garlic soup, *Campbell's®*
½	cup sour cream

1. In a 5-quart slow cooker, combine onion and mushrooms.

2. Season chicken thighs with salt, pepper, and one teaspoon paprika. Place in slow cooker on top of the vegetables.

3. In a small bowl, stir together cream of mushroom soup and remaining one tablespoon of paprika. Pour over chicken.

4. Cover and cook on LOW setting for 3½ to 4½ hours.

5. Remove chicken from slow cooker and keep warm. Strain and defat cooking liquid. Stir sour cream into liquid and serve hot over chicken.

Tomato-Garlic Chicken

Prep 10 minutes
Cook Low 3½ to 4½ hours
Servings 4

2	zucchinis, sliced into ¼-inch-thick rounds
1	cup frozen chopped onions, *Ore-Ida*®
1	can (28-ounce) whole peeled tomatoes, coarsely broken into pieces, *Muir Glen*®
10	whole peeled garlic cloves, *Christopher Ranch*®
4	boneless skinless chicken breasts, rinsed and patted dry
	Salt and pepper
1	packet (1.6-ounce) garlic herb sauce mix, *Knorr*®
1	can (6-ounce) tomato paste, *Contadina*®
½	cup olive tapenade, *Cantare*®
½	cup low sodium chicken broth, *Swanson*®

1. In a 5-quart slow cooker, combine zucchinis, onions, tomatoes, and garlic.

2. Season chicken breasts with salt and pepper. Place in slow cooker on top of vegetables.

3. In a small bowl, stir together garlic herb sauce mix, tomato paste, tapenade, and chicken broth. Pour over chicken.

4. Cover and cook on LOW setting for 3½ to 4½ hours.

Thai Peanut Chicken

Prep 5 minutes
Cook Low 3½ to 4½ hours
Servings 6

A spirited combo of coconut milk, peanut butter, and lime juice headline a sensory sauce that's just the right blend of sweet and tart. It's a good dish for company, producing a definite wow factor as guests walk in the door.

1½ cups converted rice, uncooked, *Uncle Ben's*®
6 boneless skinless chicken thighs, cut into 1-inch pieces
1 can (14.5-ounce) low sodium chicken broth, *Swanson*®
1 can (14-ounce) coconut milk, *Thai Kitchen*®
2 tablespoons Thai seasoning, *Spice Islands*®
5 tablespoons creamy peanut butter, *Skippy*®
2 tablespoons lime juice, *ReaLime*®
2 scallions, sliced, plus extra for garnish

1. Place rice in the bottom of a 4-or 5-quart slow cooker. Add chicken.

2. In a large bowl, whisk together all remaining ingredients. Pour mixture into slow cooker and stir thoroughly.

3. Cover and cook on LOW setting for 3½ to 4½ hours.

Serving ideas: Garnish with sliced scallion and wedges of fresh lime.

Sake Chicken with Edamame

Prep 8 minutes
Cook Low 3½ to 4½ hours
Servings 4

1 cup sliced fresh mushrooms
1 bag (16-ounce) frozen shelled edamame
1 cup chopped baby carrots
4 boneless skinless chicken breasts, rinsed and patted dry
3 teaspoons Szechwan seasoning, divided, *Spice Islands*®
½ cup sake
2 teaspoons soy sauce, *Kikkoman*®
1¼ cups low-sodium chicken broth, *Swanson*®
2 tablespoons lemon juice, *ReaLemon*®
2 scallions, sliced, plus extra for garnish

1. In the bottom of a 5-quart slow cooker, combine mushrooms, edamame, and carrots.

2. Season chicken breasts with one teaspoon Szechwan seasoning. Place in slow cooker on top of vegetables.

3. In a small bowl, whisk together sake, soy sauce, chicken broth, lemon juice, scallions, and remaining two teaspoons of Szechwan seasoning. Pour over chicken.

4. Cover and cook on LOW setting for 3½ to 4½ hours.

Serving ideas: Serve over white rice, garnished with scallions.

Chicken with Spiced Figs

Prep 5 minutes
Cook Low 3½ to 4½ hours
Servings 4

Figs have more fiber than any other fruit, so pairing them with chicken breasts makes a health-smart choice. Balsamic vinegar smells pungent, but it actually sweetens the dish, working with ginger and pumpkin pie spices to intensify flavor.

1½	cups frozen pearl onions, *C&W*®
4	boneless skinless chicken breasts, rinsed and patted dry
1	teaspoon salt
1½	teaspoons salt-free lemon pepper, *McCormick*®
1	cup dried Mission figs, *Sun-Maid*®
1	cup low-sodium chicken broth, *Swanson*®
½	cup ginger preserves, *Robertson's*®
2	teaspoons pumpkin pie spice, *McCormick*®
2	tablespoons balsamic vinegar

1. Place pearl onions in the bottom of a 4-or 5-quart slow cooker.

2. Season both sides of chicken breasts with salt and lemon pepper. Place in slow cooker on top of onions, and add the figs.

3. In a medium bowl, stir together all remaining ingredients and pour over chicken.

4. Cover and cook on LOW setting for 3½ to 4½ hours.

Turkey with Leeks and Mushrooms

Prep 5 minutes
Cook Low 3½ to 4½ hours
Servings 4

2   leeks, white part only, cleaned well, and sliced widthwise, ½-inch thick
1   package (8-ounce) sliced fresh mushrooms
2   pounds turkey breast cutlets, rinsed and patted dry
      Salt and pepper
1   can (10¾-ounce) condensed cream of mushroom soup, *Campbell's*®
1   packet (0.75-ounce) mushroom gravy mix, *French's*®
½   cup white wine, Chardonnay

1. In a 5-quart slow cooker, place leeks and mushrooms. Season turkey breasts with salt and pepper. Place in slow cooker on top of vegetables.

2. In a small bowl, stir together cream of mushroom soup, gravy mix, and white wine until smooth. Pour over turkey.

3. Cover and cook on LOW setting for 3½ to 4½ hours.

Broccoli-Rice Stuffed Turkey Breast

Prep 10 minutes
Cook Low 3½ to 4½ hours
Servings 4

1   medium onion, peeled and sliced
¾   cup frozen chopped broccoli, thawed, *C&W*®
¾   cup precooked long grain and wild ready rice, *Uncle Ben's*®
2   cans (10 ounces each) condensed cream of broccoli soup, divided, *Campbell's*®
1   boneless skinless turkey breast, rinsed and patted dry
1   teaspoon garlic salt, *Lawry's*®
¾   teaspoon ground black pepper
1   teaspoon crushed garlic, *Christopher Ranch*®
½   cup white wine, Chardonnay

1. Place sliced onion in the bottom of a 5-quart slow cooker.

2. Finely chop thawed broccoli and transfer to a small bowl. Add rice and three tablespoons of cream of broccoli soup. Stir to combine and set aside.

3. Cut a pocket into the turkey breast, being careful not to cut all the way through. Spoon broccoli-rice mixture into the pocket and secure with toothpicks.

4. Season both sides of turkey breast with garlic salt and pepper. Insert a pop-up thermometer in the thickest part of the breast. Place in slow cooker on top of onions.

5. In a medium bowl, stir together the remaining soup, garlic, and white wine. Pour over stuffed turkey breast. Cover and cook on LOW setting for 3½ to 4½ hours, checking to see that thermometer has popped up.

6. Remove turkey breast and tent with aluminum foil. Allow to rest for 5 to 10 minutes before slicing.

Serving ideas: Slice breast and serve hot with sauce and onions.

Turkey with Saffron Nut Sauce

Prep 10 minutes
Cook Low 3½ to 4½ hours
Servings 4

1	cup frozen chopped onions, *Ore-Ida*®
¼	cup sweet cream sherry, *Christian Brothers*®
1	pinch saffron threads
1	cup nut topping, *Diamond*®
2	tablespoons butter, melted
2	pounds turkey breast cutlets, rinsed and patted dry
	Salt and pepper
½	teaspoon paprika, *McCormick*®
1	can (10.5-ounce) white sauce, *Aunt Penny's*®
2	tablespoons lemon juice, *ReaLemon*®

1. Place onions in the bottom of a 5-quart slow cooker.

2. In a small bowl, combine sherry and saffron threads. In a different bowl, combine nut topping and melted butter.

3. Season turkey cutlets with salt, pepper, and paprika. Lay cutlets flat and press nut mixture into the middle of each and fold over. Place in slow cooker on top of onions.

4. In a medium bowl, whisk together white sauce, sherry with saffron threads, and lemon juice. Pour over turkey.

5. Cover and cook on LOW setting for 3½ to 4½ hours.

Orange-Bourbon Turkey Tenders

Prep 8 minutes
Cook Low 3 to 4 hours
Servings 4

2	pounds turkey breast tenders, rinsed and patted dry
	Salt and pepper
2	cans (10½ ounces each) mandarin orange sections in juice, drained, juice reserved, *S&W®*
3	tablespoons frozen orange juice concentrate, *Minute Maid®*
¼	cup bourbon, *Jim Beam®*
2	tablespoons light brown sugar, *C&H®*
2	tablespoons cold butter, cut into 4 chunks

1. Season turkey tenders with salt and pepper. Place in the bottom of a 5-quart slow cooker and add orange sections.

2. In a medium bowl, whisk reserved juice from orange sections, orange juice concentrate, bourbon, and brown sugar. Pour into slow cooker and stir thoroughly.

3. Cover and cook on LOW setting for 3 to 4 hours.

4. Using a slotted spoon, carefully remove turkey tenders and orange sections to a platter and keep warm. Strain liquid into a small saucepan, bring to a boil over high heat and reduce by half. Lower temperature to a simmer and whisk in cold butter chunks one at a time.

Serving ideas: Serve turkey hot with sauce.

Creamy Turkey in Puff Pastry

Prep 8 minutes
Cook Low 3½ to 4½ hours
Servings 6

Everyday turkey becomes dinner party worthy in a fashionable puff pastry that's easily made with frozen pastry shells. A fruity Chardonnay, mushrooms, and pearl onions make a refined sauce.

2	pounds turkey breast cutlets, cut into bite-sized pieces
1½	cups sliced fresh mushrooms
1	cup frozen pearl onions, *C&W*®
1	fennel bulb, diced, top removed
1	teaspoon crushed garlic, *Christopher Ranch*®
1	tablespoon Herbes de Provence, *McCormick*®
1	can (10-ounce) condensed cream of mushroom soup, *Campbell's*®
½	cup white wine, Chardonnay
1	teaspoon salt
½	teaspoon fresh ground black pepper
1	box (10-ounce) frozen puff pastry shells, *Pepperidge Farm*®

1. In a large bowl, stir together all ingredients except the puff pastry shells. Transfer to a 4-or 5-quart slow cooker.

2. Cover and cook on LOW setting for 3½ to 4½ hours.

3. A half hour before serving, preheat oven to 400 degrees F. Cook pastry shells according to package instructions.

4. Serve pastry shells filled with creamy turkey and topped with pastry lid.

Turkey Breast in Roasted Red Bell Pepper BBQ Sauce

Prep 8 minutes
Cook Low 3½ to 4½ hours
Servings 4

1	medium sweet onion, peeled and sliced
1	boneless skinless turkey breast, rinsed and patted dry
1	teaspoon salt
1	teaspoon ground black pepper
2	teaspoons salt-free chicken seasoning, *McCormick Grill Mates®*
1	cup BBQ Sauce, *Bull's Eye®*
1	cup roasted red bell peppers, *Dellalo®*
2	tablespoons red wine vinegar

1. Place onion in a 5-quart slow cooker.

2. Season turkey breast with salt, pepper, and chicken seasoning. Insert a pop-up thermometer in the thickest part of the breast. Place in slow cooker on top of onion.

3. In a blender or food processor, combine BBQ sauce, red bell peppers, and vinegar. Blend until smooth. Pour over turkey breast.

4. Cover and cook on LOW setting for 3½ to 4½ hours, checking to see that thermometer has popped up.

Tuscan Turkey Meatloaf

Prep 10 minutes
Cook High 1 hour, **Low** 5 to 6 hours
Servings 6

In Italy, they call it polpettone, which means "big meatball." This version replaces ground beef with a more delicate-tasting ground turkey that receives an herby boost from sun-dried tomatoes and a Cabernet marinara sauce.

1	medium onion, peeled and sliced thick
2½	pounds ground turkey
1	packet (0.7-ounce) Italian salad dressing mix, divided, *Good Seasons*®
½	cup julienned sun-dried tomatoes in oil, drained, *California*®
½	cup Italian cheese crumbles, *Kraft*®
¾	cup Italian bread crumbs
2	eggs
2	tablespoons balsamic vinegar
1¾	cups Cabernet marinara sauce, divided, *Classico*®
¾	teaspoon salt

1. Place onion in a 5-quart slow cooker.

2. In a large bowl, combine ground turkey, half of the salad dressing mix, sun-dried tomatoes, cheese crumbles, bread crumbs, eggs, balsamic vinegar, ¾ cup marinara sauce, and salt. With wooden spoon or clean hands, mix thoroughly and form into a loaf.

3. Place loaf in slow cooker on top of the onion, making sure meatloaf does not touch the sides of the slow cooker.

4. In a small bowl, stir together remaining marinara sauce and remaining salad dressing mix. Pour over meatloaf.

5. Cover and cook on HIGH setting for 1 hour. Lower temperature to LOW setting and cook for an additional 5 to 6 hours.

Tip: Always remember to thoroughly wash your hands after working with raw poultry, meat, or pork.

Hearty Soups and Stews

Vichyssoise. Consommé. Le potage. A soup by any other name is still a bowl full of nurturing. By the age of 15, I'd learned that one can of soup spells endless possibilities. Swap milk for water and tomato soup becomes a light lunch. Stir in chunks of beef and vegetables and it becomes a hearty supper. Add clams and herbs and it's elegant enough for company.

This chapter bubbles over with soups of every taste and texture. The trick is to start with a canned soup stock, layer in flavors, then cook it low and slow to let the tastes intermingle. Posole con Tequila calls on cilantro and jalapeños to give cubed pork a spicy spin. Beef Stew with Chocolate adds a bittersweet note to an old family faithful. After Hours Soup turns a breakfast food buffet into a 24/7 eye-opener. Dish them up plain or add toppings as an extra flavor enhancer—either way, it's a souper meal.

The Recipes

Chicken Edamame Chowder

Prep 3 minutes
Cook High 3 to 4 hours
Servings 6

Edamame (soybeans) are a wonder food, containing all the amino acids our bodies need. Combined with corn, potatoes, and chicken tenders, they pack a day's worth of protein in a single serving.

1¼	pounds chicken tenders, cut into bite-sized pieces
2	cans (14.75 ounces each) cream-style corn, *Green Giant®*
3	cups frozen shelled edamame
2	cups diced potatoes, *Reser's®*
½	cup frozen chopped onions, *Ore-Ida®*
¼	cup crumbled bacon, *Hormel®*
2	cups low-sodium chicken broth, *Swanson®*
½	cup half-and-half
	Salt and pepper

1. In a 4-quart slow cooker, combine all ingredients except half-and-half and salt and pepper. Mix thoroughly.

2. Cover and cook on HIGH setting for 3 to 4 hours.

3. Before serving, stir in half-and-half and adjust seasoning with salt and pepper. Serve hot.

Posole con Tequila

Prep 5 minutes
Cook High 3 to 4 hours
Servings 6

1	pound pork tenderloin, cut into bite-sized pieces
2	cans (15 ounces each) white hominy
1	packet (1.25-ounce) white chicken chili seasoning, *McCormick®*
1	can (7-ounce) diced green chiles, *Ortega®*
½	cup sliced jalapeños, *Ortega®*
1	cup frozen chopped onions, *Ore-Ida®*
½	cup silver tequila, *Jose Cuervo®*
3	cups low-sodium chicken broth, *Swanson®*
2	tablespoons chopped fresh cilantro, for garnish
	Salt and pepper

1. In a 4-quart slow cooker, combine all ingredients except cilantro and salt and pepper, and mix thoroughly.

2. Cover and cook on HIGH setting for 3 to 4 hours.

3. Stir in cilantro and adjust seasoning with salt and pepper. Serve hot.

Serving ideas: Garnish with additional cilantro and lime wedges.

Surfer Soup

Prep 5 minutes
Cook High 3 to 4 hours
Servings 6

They call them fruits de mer—fruits of the sea. Whole shrimp, fresh cod, and cabbage leaves float in a pretty shrimp bisque, with diced jalapeños, garlic, onions, and tequila lime salsa to give it bite.

2   cans (10 ounces each) condensed cream of shrimp soup, *Campbell's®*
2   bottles (8 ounces each) clam juice, *Snow's®*
1   jar (16-ounce) tequila lime salsa, *Newman's Own®*
1   teaspoon crushed garlic, *Christopher Ranch®*
1   tablespoon salt-free Mexican seasoning, *The Spice Hunter®*
1   tablespoon diced jalapeños, *Ortega®*
1   cup frozen chopped onion, *Ore-Ida®*
2   cups green cabbage leaves, cut into 1-inch dice
1   pound fresh cod, cut into 1-inch pieces
1   bag (12-ounce) frozen medium shrimp
   Salt and pepper

1. In a 4-quart slow cooker, combine shrimp soup, clam juice, salsa, garlic, and Mexican seasoning and stir well. Add jalapeños, onions, and cabbage. Mix thoroughly.

2. Cover and cook on HIGH setting for 3 to 4 hours.

3. Add cod and shrimp. Cook for an additional hour.

4. Adjust seasoning with salt and pepper. Serve hot.

Serving Ideas: Garnish with a dollop of sour cream and chopped fresh cilantro.

After Hours Soup

Prep 5 minutes
Cook High 4 hours
Servings 6

1	package (16-ounce) hot Italian sausage, cut into bite-sized pieces
2	cups diced potatoes, *Reser's®*
½	cup cooked and crumbled bacon, *Hormel®*
1	can (14.5-ounce) diced tomatoes, *Muir Glen®*
4	cups low-sodium chicken broth, *Swanson®*
2	teaspoons chopped garlic, *Christopher Ranch®*
1	packet (0.9-ounce) Hollandaise sauce mix, *Knorr®*
4	eggs, scrambled
	Salt and pepper
2	cups large croutons (or cubed leftover bread)
	Tabasco® sauce, optional

1. In a 4-quart slow cooker, combine sausage, potatoes, bacon, and tomatoes.

2. In a medium bowl, whisk together chicken broth, garlic, and Hollandaise mix. Pour into slow cooker and stir thoroughly. Cover and cook on HIGH setting for 4 hours.

3. Slowly stir in the scrambled eggs and adjust seasoning with salt and pepper.

4. Top with croutons and serve hot with Tabasco sauce, if desired.

Curried Pork Stew

Prep 10 minutes
Cook High 4 to 6 hours
Servings 6

1	pound boneless pork loin, cut into bite-sized pieces
1	medium onion, peeled and diced
1	cup diced potatoes, *Reser's®*
2	cans (8 ounces each) pineapple chunks, drained, *Dole®*
4	cups vegetable stock, *Kitchen Basics®*
1	package (3.5-ounce) golden curry mix (brick), *S&B®*
2	teaspoons crushed garlic, *Christopher Ranch®*
2	teaspoons chopped ginger, *Christopher Ranch®*
	Salt and pepper

1. In a 4-quart slow cooker, combine pork, onion, potatoes, and pineapple chunks.

2. Heat vegetable stock in the microwave. In a large bowl, combine the hot stock, curry mix, garlic, and ginger. Stir until curry mix is dissolved. Pour into slow cooker and stir thoroughly.

3. Cover and cook on HIGH setting for 4 to 6 hours.

4. Adjust seasoning with salt and pepper. Serve hot.

Beef Stew with Chocolate

Prep 10 minutes
Cook High 4 to 6 hours
Servings 6

2	pounds beef stew meat, cut into bite-sized pieces
1	package (8-ounce) sliced brown mushrooms
1	leek, white part only, cut in half lengthwise, cleaned well, and sliced widthwise
3	cups diced red seasoned potatoes, *Reser's*®
1	can (14.5-ounce) diced tomatoes, *Muir Glen*®
1	cup frozen sliced carrots, *Pictsweet*®
1	ounce bittersweet chocolate, finely grated, *Ghirardelli*®
1	packet (1.5-ounce) meatloaf seasoning, *McCormick*®
1	teaspoon crushed garlic, *Christopher Ranch*®
1	can (14-ounce) low-sodium beef broth, *Swanson*®
1	cup red wine, Merlot
	Salt and pepper

1. In a 4-quart slow cooker, combine beef, mushrooms, leeks, potatoes, tomatoes, and carrots.

2. In a medium bowl, stir together grated chocolate, meatloaf seasoning packet, garlic, beef broth, and red wine. Pour into slow cooker and stir thoroughly.

3. Cover and cook on HIGH setting for 4 to 6 hours.

4. Adjust seasoning with salt and pepper. Serve hot.

Spicy Pork Stew with Clams

Prep 5 minutes
Cook High 4 to 6 hours
Servings 6

1	pound pork tenderloin, cut into bite-sized pieces
1	pound hot Italian sausage, cut into bite-sized pieces
2	cans (6.5 ounces each) minced clams in juice, *Snow's®*
1	cup frozen chopped onions, *Ore-Ida®*
1	cup diced potatoes, *Reser's®*
1	jar (12-ounce) roasted red peppers, drained, *Delallo®*
1	package (10-ounce) frozen leaf spinach, thawed
1	can (6-ounce) tomato paste, *Contadina®*
1	teaspoon red pepper flakes
2	tablespoons garlic herb sauce mix, *Knorr®*
1	cup white wine, Chardonnay
3	cups low-sodium chicken broth, *Swanson®*
	Salt and pepper

1. In a 4-quart slow cooker, combine pork, sausage, clams, onions, potatoes, red peppers, and spinach.

2. In a large bowl, whisk together the remaining ingredients except salt and pepper. Pour into slow cooker and stir thoroughly.

3. Cover and cook on HIGH setting for 4 to 6 hours.

4. Adjust seasoning with salt and pepper. Serve hot.

Russian Pork Stew

Prep 5 minutes
Cook High 4 to 6 hours
Servings 8

3	pounds boneless pork shoulder, trimmed and cut into bite-sized pieces
	Salt and pepper
1	bag (16-ounce) frozen sliced carrots, *Pictsweet*
1	bag (14-ounce) frozen pearl onions, *C&W*
1	cup dried apricots, *Sun-Maid*
1	cup dried pitted prunes, *Sunsweet*
4	cups low sodium chicken broth, *Swanson*
2	packets (1 ounce each) peppercorn sauce mix, *Knorr*
1	can (6-ounce) tomato paste, *Contadina*

1. Season pork pieces with salt and pepper to taste and place in a 5-quart slow cooker. Add carrots, onions, apricots, and prunes. Stir to combine.

2. In a medium bowl, stir together chicken broth, peppercorn sauce mix, and tomato paste. Pour into slow cooker and stir thoroughly.

3. Cover and cook on HIGH setting for 4 to 6 hours.

4. Adjust seasoning with salt and pepper. Serve hot.

Hearty Soups and Stews | 135

Hearty Beef and Root Vegetable Stew

Prep 10 minutes
Cook High 4 to 6 hours
Servings 6

2	pounds beef stew meat, cut into bite-sized pieces
	Salt and pepper
2	parsnips, peeled and diced
1	leek, white part only, cut in half lengthwise, cleaned well, and sliced widthwise
2	celery ribs, diced
1½	cups frozen sliced carrots, *Birds Eye*®
2	cups diced potatoes, *Reser's*®
1	can (28-ounce) whole peeled tomatoes, each cut in half, juice reserved, *Muir Glen*®
½	tablespoon crushed garlic, *Christopher Ranch*®
1	can (14-ounce) low-sodium beef broth, *Swanson*®
1	packet (1.5-ounce) meatloaf seasoning, *McCormick*®

1. Season stew meat with salt and pepper to taste. Place stew meat, parsnips, leeks, celery, carrots, potatoes, and tomatoes in a 5-quart slow cooker.

2. In a small bowl, whisk together juice from tomatoes, garlic, beef broth, and meatloaf seasoning. Pour liquid into slow cooker and stir thoroughly.

3. Cover and cook on HIGH setting for 4 to 6 hours.

4. Adjust seasoning with salt and pepper. Serve hot.

South-of-the-Border Beef Stew

Prep 10 minutes
Cook High 4 to 6 hours
Servings 6

Ranchero tomato soup is the base for a stew as peppy as a Mariachi band. Chock-full of beef chunks, potatoes, and corn kernels, it receives its intense flavor from salsa, onions, and a cup of Corona®.

2	pounds beef stew meat, cut into bite-sized pieces
	Salt and pepper
2	cups diced potatoes, *Reser's®*
1	cup frozen corn kernels, *C&W®*
1	small onion, peeled and chopped
1	jar (16-ounce) chunky salsa, *Pace®*
1	can (10¾-ounce) condensed creamy ranchero tomato soup, *Campbell's®*
1	cup low-sodium beef broth, *Swanson®*
1	cup beer, *Corona®*

1. Season stew meat with salt and pepper to taste. Place in a 4-quart slow cooker. Add potatoes, corn, onion, and salsa. Stir to combine.

2. In a medium bowl, stir together ranchero tomato soup, beef broth, and beer. Pour into slow cooker and stir thoroughly. Cover and cook on HIGH setting for 4 to 6 hours.

3. Adjust seasoning with salt and pepper. Serve hot.

White Stew

Prep 8 minutes
Cook High 4 to 6 hours
Servings 6

White foods are comfort food, and this thick, creamy stew has them all—potatoes, white corn, and cannellini beans, mixed with turkey breast in a garlicky chicken-potato broth. To dress it up, sprinkle bits of parsley or grated cheese on top.

1¼	**pounds turkey breast cutlets, cut into strips**
2	**parsnips, peeled and sliced**
1	**cup diced potatoes, *Reser's*®**
1	**cup frozen white corn kernels, *C&W*®**
2	**packages (8 ounces each) sliced white button mushrooms**
1	**can (15-ounce) cannellini beans, *Progresso*®**
1	**packet (1.6-ounce) garlic herb sauce mix, *Knorr*®**
1	**can (10¾-ounce) condensed cream of potato soup, *Campbell's*®**
2	**cups low-sodium chicken broth, *Swanson*®**
	Salt and white pepper

1. In a 4-quart slow cooker, combine turkey strips, parsnips, potatoes, white corn, mushrooms, and beans.

2. In a small bowl, whisk together garlic herb sauce mix, cream of potato soup, and chicken broth. Pour into slow cooker and stir thoroughly.

3. Cover and cook on HIGH setting for 4 to 6 hours.

4. Adjust seasoning with salt and white pepper. Serve hot.

Irish Stew

Prep 10 minutes
Cook High 4 to 6 hours
Servings 6

1½	pounds boneless lamb shoulder or lamb stew meat, cut into bite-sized pieces
1½	cups baby carrots, cut into ½-inch pieces
1½	cups frozen pearl onions, *C&W*®
2	cups seasoned diced potatoes, *Reser's*®
2	cans (10 ounces each) condensed cream of potato soup, *Campbell's*®
1	cup *Guinness Stout*®
	Salt and pepper

1. In a 4-quart slow cooker, place lamb, carrots, onions, and potatoes.

2. In a medium bowl, stir together the potato soup and beer. Pour into slow cooker and stir thoroughly.

3. Cover and cook on HIGH setting for 4 to 6 hours. Adjust seasoning with salt and pepper. Serve hot.

Meat

It's little wonder the French call their English brethren les rosbifs—Sunday roast has been an institution in Britain for centuries. Maybe it's our British roots or maybe it's the cozy convenience of cooking meat, vegetables, and gravy all in one pot, but roast meat has outlasted many a culinary trend. Whatever day we cook it, inexpensive cuts of meats simmered at leisure in a seasoned broth are a sure thing in the food world.

This chapter is a menu of three-way meats that can be served alone or over rice, pasta, or even a pita. Give traditional roast beef a fiesta of flavor with black beans and salsa. Go gourmet with pork in a ginger-lime sauce or veal served Mediterranean-style with green olives and garlic. Even meatloaf is reinvented for the slow cooker with healthy ground pork and lamb. Pillow it on a bed of mashed potatoes with sauce ladled over the top and the tradition, like the flavor, will never fade.

The Recipes

Ginger-Lime Pork

Prep 5 minutes
Cook Low 8 to 10 hours
Servings 6

1	medium onion, peeled and sliced
3	pounds boneless pork butt, rinsed and patted dry
3	tablespoons salt-free Thai seasoning, *The Spice Hunter*®
½	cup sake
½	cup ginger preserves, *Robertson's*®
2	tablespoons chopped jalapeños, *La Victoria*®
2	tablespoons soy sauce, *Kikkoman*®
2	tablespoons lime juice, *ReaLime*®

1. Place onions in a 5-quart slow cooker.

2. Season all sides of pork butt with Thai seasoning. Place in slow cooker on top of onions, fat side up.

3. In a small bowl, stir together remaining ingredients and pour over pork butt. Cover and cook on LOW setting for 8 to 10 hours.

Serving ideas: Garnish this succulent Indonesian dish with wedges of fresh lime.

Apricot and Tarragon Pork Chops

Prep 5 minutes
Cook Low 4 to 5 hours
Servings 4

2	medium onions, each one peeled and cut into eights through core
1	bag (6-ounce) dried apricots, *Mariani*®
4	boneless, thick-cut, pork loin chops, rinsed and patted dry
1½	teaspoons garlic salt, *McCormick*®
1	teaspoon ground black pepper
1	can (10-ounce) condensed cream of celery soup, *Campbell's*®
¾	cup apricot preserves, *Knott's Berry Farm*®
1	tablespoon dried tarragon, *McCormick*®

1. Place onions and dried apricots in a 5-quart slow cooker.

2. Season pork chops with garlic salt and black pepper. Place on top of the onions.

3. In a small bowl, stir together cream of celery soup, apricot preserves, and dried tarragon. Pour over the pork chops.

4. Cover and cook on LOW setting for 4 to 5 hours.

5. Strain and defat the cooking liquid. Serve as sauce on the side.

Pork Roast with Whiskey Sauce

Prep 5 minutes
Cook Low 8 to 10 hours
Servings 6

1	medium onion, peeled and sliced
3½	pounds boneless pork butt, rinsed and patted dry
1	tablespoon Montreal steak seasoning, *McCormick Grill Mates®*
3	tablespoons frozen orange juice concentrate, *Minute Maid®*
½	cup whiskey, *Jack Daniels®*
2	tablespoons salt-free citrus herb seasoning, *Spice Islands®*
¼	cup Dijon mustard, *Grey Poupon®*

1. Place onion in a 5-quart slow cooker.

2. Season all sides of pork butt with Montreal steak seasoning. Place in slow cooker on top of onions, fat side up.

3. In a small bowl, stir together remaining ingredients. Pour over pork roast. Cover and cook on LOW setting for 8 to 10 hours.

4. Strain and defat cooking liquid. Serve as sauce on the side.

Chinese BBQ Pork

Prep 5 minutes
Cook Low 8 to 10 hours
Servings 6

2	cups frozen chopped onions, *Ore-Ida*®
3	pounds boneless pork shoulder, rinsed and patted dry
1	teaspoon salt
1	teaspoon ground black pepper
1	cup hoisin sauce, *Lee Kum Kee*®
¼	cup chili sauce, *Heinz*®
2	tablespoons honey, *Sue Bee*®
1	teaspoon Chinese 5-spice powder, *McCormick*® *Gourmet*
1	tablespoon minced ginger, *Christopher Ranch*®
2	teaspoons crushed garlic, *Christopher Ranch*®

1. Place onions in a 5-quart slow cooker.

2. Season pork shoulder with salt and pepper. Place in slow cooker on top of onions, fat side up. In a small bowl, stir together the remaining ingredients and pour over pork shoulder.

3. Cover and cook on LOW setting for 8 to 10 hours.

4. Strain and defat cooking liquid. Serve as sauce on the side.

Serving ideas: Serve with bowls of steamed white rice.

Pork with Sherried Plantains

Prep 8 minutes
Cook Low 5 to 6 hours
Servings 4

Tropical plantains are less mushy and lower in sugar than their cousin, the banana. Slow-roasted with pork in a sherried brown sugar-cinnamon sauce, it's simple enough for a weeknight, yet special enough for guests.

4	plantains, peeled and sliced ¼-inch thick
6	tablespoons butter, cut into small pieces
2	tablespoons light brown sugar
1	teaspoon ground cinnamon, *McCormick®*
2	tablespoons frozen orange juice concentrate, *Minute Maid®*
½	cup cream sherry, *Christian Brothers®*
1	tablespoon salt-free citrus herb seasoning, *Spice Islands®*
1	teaspoon garlic salt, *Lawry's®*
1	teaspoon salt-free lemon pepper, *McCormick®*
4	boneless, thick-cut pork loin chops, rinsed and patted dry

1. In a 4-or 5-quart slow cooker, combine plantains, butter, brown sugar, cinnamon, orange juice concentrate, and cream sherry. Toss to coat plantains.

2. In a small bowl, combine citrus herb seasoning, garlic salt, and lemon pepper. Season pork chops with mixture. Place chops in slow cooker on top of plantains.

3. Cover and cook on LOW setting for 5 to 6 hours.

4. Strain and defat cooking liquid. Serve as sauce on the side.

Spanish-Style Veal Shoulder with Green Olives

Prep 8 minutes
Cook Low 6 to 8 hours
Servings 4

1½	cups frozen pepper strips, *Birds Eye*®
1	cup frozen chopped onions, *Ore-Ida*®
1	cup frozen sliced carrots, *Birds Eye*®
1	can (15-ounce) diced tomatoes, drained, *Muir Glen*®
12	whole peeled garlic cloves, *Christopher Ranch*®
2½	pounds veal shoulder, rinsed and patted dry
1	teaspoon garlic salt, *Lawry's*®
1	teaspoon ground black pepper
1	can (10-ounce) condensed tomato soup, *Campbell's*®
¾	cup low-sodium beef broth, *Swanson*®
1	tablespoon paprika
1	jar (7-ounce) Spanish olives, drained, *Early California*®

1. In a 5-quart slow cooker, combine pepper strips, onions, carrots, tomatoes, and garlic cloves.

2. Season veal shoulder with garlic salt and pepper. Place in slow cooker on top of vegetables.

3. In a small bowl, stir together the tomato soup, beef broth, and paprika. Pour over veal shoulder. Top with Spanish olives.

4. Cover and cook on LOW setting for 6 to 8 hours. Remove veal shoulder and let rest 5 to 10 minutes before carving.

5. Strain and defat cooking liquid, reserving the olives. Reheat, return olives to the pan, and serve as sauce on the side.

Serving ideas: Serve with hunks of fresh, country-style bread.

Roast Beef with Tomato Ragout

Prep 8 minutes
Cook Low 8 to 10 hours
Servings 6

1	large red onion, peeled and sliced thin
1	can (28-ounce) whole peeled tomatoes with basil, drained, broken into pieces, *Progresso*®
3	pounds beef rump roast, rinsed and patted dry
1	teaspoon garlic salt, *Lawry's*®
1	teaspoon ground black pepper
1	can (10-ounce) condensed tomato soup, *Campbell's*®
2	tablespoons balsamic vinegar
1	envelope (1.1-ounce) beefy onion soup mix, *Lipton*®
1	tablespoon Italian seasoning, *McCormick*®
1	teaspoon crushed garlic, *Christopher Ranch*®

1. In a 5-quart slow cooker, combine onion and tomatoes.

2. Season rump roast with garlic salt and pepper. Place roast in slow cooker on top of vegetables, fat side up.

3. In a small bowl, stir together remaining ingredients thoroughly and pour over rump roast.

4. Cover and cook on LOW setting for 8 to 10 hours.

5. Strain and defat cooking liquid. Serve as sauce on the side.

Balsamic Veal Roast with Grapes

Prep 8 minutes
Cook Low 6 to 8 hours
Servings 4

1	bag (16-ounce) frozen pearl onions, *C&W*®
2½	pounds veal shoulder roast, rinsed and patted dry
1	teaspoon garlic salt, *Lawry's*®
1	teaspoon ground black pepper
1½	cups low-sodium chicken broth, *Swanson*®
⅓	cup balsamic vinegar
1	packet (1.8-ounce) leek soup mix, *Knorr*®
1	pound red seedless grapes, washed and stems removed, ½ cup reserved for garnish

1. Place pearl onions in a 5-quart slow cooker.

2. Season veal roast with garlic salt and pepper. Place in slow cooker on top of pearl onions.

3. In a small bowl, whisk together chicken broth, balsamic vinegar, and leek soup mix. Pour over veal roast.

4. Top the veal roast with grapes. Cover and cook on LOW setting for 6 to 8 hours.

Serving ideas: Garnish with reserved grapes.

New Mexico Beef Roast

Prep 8 minutes
Cook Low 8 to 10 hours
Servings 6

1	package (4 count) mixed bell peppers, seeded, veined, and cut into ½-inch-thick strips, *Ready Pac*®
1	large red onion, peeled and sliced
3½	pounds chuck roast, rinsed and patted dry
1	packet (1.25-ounce) southwest marinade mix, *McCormick Grill Mates*®
1	jar (16-ounce) black bean and corn salsa, *Ortega*®
1	can (10-ounce) condensed creamy ranchero tomato soup, *Campbell's*®

1. In the bottom of a 5-quart slow cooker, combine peppers and onion.

2. Season all sides of chuck roast with southwest marinade mix. Place in slow cooker on top of vegetables.

3. In a small bowl, stir together salsa and tomato soup. Pour in slow cooker over chuck roast.

4. Cover and cook on LOW setting for 8 to 10 hours.

Bourbon-Mustard Brisket

Prep 8 minutes
Cook Low 12 to 14 hours
Servings 6

Brisket tends to be tough, but slow-simmering it in a **Low Country** bourbon mustard broth makes it fall-off-the-fork tender. A brown sugar BBQ sauce balances the spicy mustard to keep the bold flavors in check.

2	large sweet onions, peeled and sliced thick
4	pounds beef brisket, rinsed and patted dry
2	teaspoons garlic salt, *Lawry's*®
2	teaspoons salt-free lemon pepper, *McCormick*®
¾	cup spicy brown mustard, *Gulden's*®
½	cup honey brown sugar BBQ sauce, *Jack Daniels*®
¼	cup bourbon
½	cup light brown sugar, *C&H*®

1. Place onions in a 5-quart slow cooker.

2. Season brisket with garlic salt and lemon pepper and place on top of the onions, cutting to fit if necessary.

3. In a small bowl, stir together remaining ingredients and pour in slow cooker over brisket. Cover and cook on LOW setting for 12 to 14 hours.

4. Strain and defat cooking liquid. Serve as sauce on the side.

Gingered Beef

Prep 5 minutes
Cook Low 12 to 14 hours
Servings 6

2	sweet onions, peeled and sliced thick
½	cup golden raisins, *Sun-Maid*®
3	tablespoons crystallized ginger, *McCormick*® *Gourmet*
4	pounds beef brisket, rinsed and patted dry
	Salt and pepper
1	cup pitted prunes, *Sunsweet*®
1	cup low-sodium beef broth, *Swanson*®
1	jar (12-ounce) ginger preserves, *Robertson's*®
1	envelope (1-ounce) onion soup mix, *Lipton*®

1. Combine onions, raisins, and crystallized ginger in a 5-quart slow cooker.

2. Season brisket with salt and pepper and place in slow cooker on top of onions, cutting to fit if necessary.

3. In a small bowl, combine remaining ingredients and pour over brisket. Cover and cook on LOW setting for 12 to 14 hours.

4. Strain and defat cooking liquid. Serve as sauce on the side.

Osso Buco

Prep 15 minutes
Cook Low 8 to 10 hours
Servings 4

Osso Buco translates to "bone with a hole," a reference to the veal shank bone with its tasty marrow filling. For a colorful presentation, try a gremolata garnish—a snippet of parsley, garlic, and grated lemon peel.

2	cups peeled and chopped turnips
1	cup diced celery
2	cups frozen sliced carrots, *S&W*®
1	cup frozen pearl onions, *Ore-Ida*®
1	can (14.5-ounce) diced tomatoes, *Muir Glen*®
4	veal shanks, center cut, rinsed and patted dry
1	can (10¾-ounce) condensed cream of chicken soup, *Campbell's*®
½	cup low-sodium chicken broth, *Swanson*®
½	cup white wine, Chardonnay
2	tablespoons Italian herb marinade mix, *Durkee*® *Grill Creations*®

1. In a 5-quart slow cooker, combine turnips, celery, carrots, pearl onions, and tomatoes. Place veal shanks on top of vegetables.

2. In a small bowl, stir together the cream of chicken soup, chicken broth, white wine, and Italian herb marinade mix. Pour in slow cooker over veal shanks.

3. Cover and cook on LOW setting for 8 to 10 hours.

Smothered Meatloaf

Prep 10 minutes
Cook High 1 hour, **Low** 5 to 6 hours
Servings 6

4	cups Potatoes O'Brien, *Ore-Ida*®
1	pound lean ground beef
1¼	pounds ground pork
1	box (5.29-ounce) garlic herb Shake 'n Bake, *Kraft* ®
1	envelope (1.1-ounce) beefy onion soup mix, *Lipton*®
1	jar (4.5-ounce) sliced mushrooms, drained, *Green Giant*®
1	egg
1	can (12-ounce) condensed cheddar soup, divided, *Campbell's*®
½	cup evaporated milk, *Carnation*®
1	can (10-ounce) condensed cream of mushroom soup, *Campbell's*®
1	medium onion, peeled and sliced thin
1	package (8-ounce) sliced fresh mushrooms

1. Place potatoes in the bottom of a 5-quart slow cooker.

2. In a large bowl, combine ground beef, ground pork, Shake 'n Bake, onion soup mix, sliced mushrooms, and egg.

3. In a small bowl, stir together ½ cup cheddar soup and evaporated milk, and add to meat mixture. Using a wooden spoon or clean hands, mix thoroughly and form into a loaf. Place in slow cooker on top of the potatoes, making sure meatloaf does not touch the sides of the slow cooker.

4. Stir together remaining cheddar soup with cream of mushroom soup. Pour over meatloaf. Top with onion and mushrooms.

5. Cover and cook on HIGH setting for 1 hour. Lower the temperature to LOW setting and cook for an additional 5 to 6 hours.

BBQ. Meatloaf

Prep 10 minutes
Cook High 1 hour, **Low** 5 to 6 hours
Servings 6

2   cups frozen seasoning blend, divided, *Pictsweet*®
2   pounds lean ground beef
½   cup bacon crumbles, *Hormel*®
1   cup seasoned bread crumbs, *Progresso*®
1   cup Hickory Smoke BBQ Sauce, divided, *Bull's-Eye*®
2   eggs
2   teaspoons Montreal steak seasoning, *McCormick Grill Mates*®
1   packet (1.31-ounce) sloppy joe seasoning, *McCormick*®
¼   cup chopped pimientos, *Dromedary*®

1. Place one cup of seasoning blend in the bottom of a 5-quart slow cooker.

2. In a large bowl, combine ground beef, bacon crumbles, bread crumbs, ½ cup BBQ sauce, eggs, Montreal steak seasoning, sloppy joe seasoning, pimientos, and remaining one cup of seasoning blend.

3. Using a wooden spoon or clean hands, mix thoroughly and form into a loaf. Place in slow cooker on top of potatoes, making sure meatloaf does not touch the sides of the slow cooker. Spread remaining BBQ sauce over meatloaf. Cover and cook on HIGH setting for 1 hour. Turn to LOW setting and cook for an additional 5 to 6 hours.

Greek Style Meatloaf

Prep 10 minutes
Cook High 1 hour, **Low** 5 to 6 hours
Servings 6

Have meatloaf for dinner and pack meatloaf sandwiches for lunch the next day. Mixing ground lamb with beef lightens it up, while feta cheese and kalamata olives capture Old World flavor. Tabouli makes it extra moist.

1   pound ground lamb
1¼   pounds ground beef
1   tablespoon Greek seasoning, *Spice Islands*®
1   package (5.25-ounce) Tabouli mix, *Near East*®
½   cup crumbled feta cheese, *Athenos*®
1   cup pitted kalamata olives, chopped, *Mezzetta*®
1   egg
1   can (8-ounce) tomato sauce with roasted garlic, *Hunt's*®

1. Make an aluminum foil ring, 1-inch thick, for soufflé dish to sit on and place inside the bottom of a 5-quart slow cooker.

2. In a large bowl, combine all ingredients. Using a wooden spoon or clean hands, mix together thoroughly and form into a round loaf. Place in 1½-quart soufflé dish. Put soufflé dish on top of foil ring in slow cooker.

3. Cover and cook on HIGH setting for 1 hour. Lower the temperature to LOW setting and cook for an additional 5 to 6 hours.

Desserts

It was called Sopa de Flor—flower soup—and its perfume was heavenly. While vacationing in Mexico, I happened upon a little out-of-the-way cantina. I opened the door and was greeted with a wonderful waft of oranges and roses. Every breath hinted of another ingredient—mint, cinnamon, berries, and bananas. The appeal wasn't any one; it was a lavish layering of flavors that was at once sweet yet spicy, familiar yet deliciously different.

Dessert in the slow cooker is like that—a silky richness telegraphed by a heady aroma. Pudding, compote, cake, or cobbler, this chapter has them all, tempting and treating you long before you lift a spoon. Bananas Foster is decadently rich, but sinfully simple, served over Oatmeal-Rum Cookies. And while Mixed Berry Crumble tastes extravagant, it's really made with calorie-conscious fruit. Bake in the slow cooker? Absolutely! Banana Chip Chocolate Cake is a beauty, cooked in a soufflé dish and iced to a finish par excellence outside.

The Recipes

Ginger Rhubarb Compote over Lemon Tartlets

Prep 10 minutes
Cook High 1½ to 2½ hours
Servings 6

FOR GINGER RHUBARB COMPOTE

2	bags (16 ounces each) frozen rhubarb, thawed and drained, *Dole*®
1	cup granulated sugar
¼	cup quick cooking tapioca, *Minute*®
1	jar (12-ounce) ginger preserves, *Robertson's*®
2	tablespoons lemon juice
¼	cup water

FOR LEMON TARTLETS

2	packages (8 ounces each) cream cheese, *Philadelphia*®
½	cup granulated sugar
1	cup lemon curd, *Dickinson's*®
1	tablespoon lemon zest
2	containters (4 ounces each) mini graham cracker pie crusts, *Keebler*®

1. Place rhubarb in a 4-quart slow cooker.

2. In a medium bowl, stir together remaining compote ingredients.

3. Pour over rhubarb. Stir thoroughly. Cover and cook on HIGH setting for 1½ to 2½ hours.

4. For tartlets, combine all tartlet ingredients, except crusts, in a large bowl. Use an electric mixer to beat on medium speed until creamy, about one minute.

5. Spread lemon mixture into mini pie crusts. Chill in refrigerator for 2 hours or until set.

Serving ideas: Serve warm Ginger Rhubarb Compote over Lemon Tartlets.

Pear and Cherry Buckle

Prep 5 minutes
Cook Low 4 to 6 hours
Servings 12

Butter-flavored cooking spray
1   can (26-ounce) cherry pie filling, *Comstock More Fruit®*
2   cans (15 ounces each) diced pears in syrup, *Del Monte®*
1   teaspoon almond extract, *McCormick®*
1   box (18.25-ounce) yellow cake mix, *Betty Crocker®*
12   tablespoons butter, cut into small pieces
1   packet (1.19-ounce) maple and brown sugar instant oatmeal, *Quaker®*
¼   cup sliced almonds, *Planters ®*
Whipped topping for serving, *Cool Whip®*

1. Spray a 5-quart slow cooker with butter-flavored cooking spray.

2. In a large bowl, combine pie filling, pears, and almond extract. Pour into prepared slow cooker. Sprinkle cake mix over fruit mixture. Dot with butter.

3. In a small bowl, combine oatmeal packet and almonds. Sprinkle over cake mixture.

4. Place 8 paper towels over slow cooker bowl and secure with lid. (This helps to trap steam.) Cook on LOW setting for 4 to 6 hours.

Serving ideas: Serve warm with whipped topping

Tip: Do not lift lid to check cake for the first 3 hours.

Sticky Date and Almond Bread Pudding

Prep 10 minutes
Cook Low 3 to 4 hours
Servings 6

Butter-flavored cooking spray
1 pound leftover or store-bought cinnamon rolls, cut into 1-inch cubes
1½ cups dried chopped dates, *Dole®*
¼ cup sliced almonds, *Planters®*
1 box (4.6-ounce) cook & serve vanilla pudding mix, *Jell-O®*
2 cans (12 ounces each) evaporated milk, *Carnation®*
½ teaspoon almond extract, *McCormick®*
½ teaspoon pumpkin pie spice, *McCormick®*
2 tablespoons butter, cut into small pieces

1. Spray the inside of a 4-or 5-quart slow cooker with butter-flavored cooking spray.

2. Place cinnamon roll cubes, dates, and almonds in a large bowl, and toss to combine thoroughly.

3. In a medium bowl, whisk together pudding mix, evaporated milk, almond extract, and pumpkin pie spice. Pour pudding mixture over bread mixture. Stir together until mixture is well combined and bread is saturated.

4. Transfer to slow cooker and dot with butter.

5. Cover and cook on LOW setting for 3 to 4 hours.

Spiced Applesauce Coffee Cake

Prep 15 minutes
Cook Low 4 to 6 hours
Servings 10

Butter-flavored cooking spray
1   box (16-ounce) pound cake mix, *Betty Crocker®*
¾   cup cinnamon applesauce, *Mott's®*
2   eggs
1   teaspoon pumpkin pie spice, *McCormick®*
½   teaspoon almond extract, *McCormick®*
¼   cup baking mix, *Bisquick®*
¾   cup chopped walnuts, *Diamond®*
1   packet (.74-ounce) spiced cider drink mix, *Alpine®*
1   tablespoon butter, melted

1. Lightly spray a 6-cup soufflé dish with butter-flavored cooking spray. Make an aluminum foil ring ½-inch thick for soufflé dish to sit on and place inside the bottom of a 5-quart slow cooker.

2. In a large bowl, combine cake mix, applesauce, eggs, pumpkin pie spice, and almond extract. Using an electric mixer, beat on low speed for 30 seconds. Scrape down sides of bowl and beat for 3 minutes on medium speed. Pour into soufflé dish and set aside.

3. In a medium bowl, stir together baking mix, walnuts, cider mix, and melted butter. Sprinkle over cake batter. Use a butter knife to cut through cake and topping several times to swirl.

4. Place soufflé dish on top of foil ring in slow cooker. Place 8 paper towels over slow cooker bowl and secure with lid. Cook on LOW setting for 4 to 6 hours or until tester comes out clean. Do not lift lid to check cake for the first 3 hours. Cool in soufflé dish on wire rack for 15 to 20 minutes before removing and slicing.

Tip: Placing 8 paper towels over slow cooker before securing with lid helps to trap steam.

Mixed Berry Crumble

Prep 10 minutes
Cook High 2 to 4 hours
Servings 8

2	bags (12 ounces each) frozen mixed berries, thawed, *Dole®*
½	cup dried cranberries, *Sun-Maid®*
⅓	cup cranberry juice cocktail, *Ocean Spray®*
¼	cup quick cooking tapioca, *Minute®*
½	teaspoon cinnamon, *McCormick®*
1	cup granulated sugar

FOR CRUMBLE TOPPING

½	cup baking mix, *Bisquick®*
¾	cup cereal, *Kashi®*
1	cup almond biscotti (about 4 to 5 cookies), crushed
2	tablespoons butter, melted

1. Combine mixed berries, dried cranberries, cranberry juice, tapioca, cinnamon, and sugar in bottom of a 4-or 5-quart slow cooker. Stir thoroughly.

2. Cover and cook on HIGH setting for 2 to 4 hours.

3. For the crumble topping, preheat oven to 350 degrees F one half hour before serving. Line a baking sheet with aluminum foil and set aside.

4. In a medium bowl, combine crumble topping ingredients. Spread out on prepared baking sheet and bake for 12 to 18 minutes or until crisp and golden brown. Sprinkle crumble topping over warm berry mixture.

Serving ideas: Serve à la mode with vanilla ice cream or with whipped topping.

Apple Rhubarb Crisp

Prep 8 minutes
Cook High 2 to 3 hours
Servings 6

1	can (20.5-ounce) apple pie filling, *Comstock More Fruit*®
1	package (16-ounce) frozen rhubarb, thawed and drained, *Dole*®
1	cup light brown sugar
¼	cup granulated sugar
1	teaspoon cinnamon
½	cup quick cooking tapioca, *Minute*®
½	cup apple juice, *Tree Top*®
2	tablespoons lemon juice, *ReaLemon*®

FOR CRISP TOPPING

½	cup baking mix, *Bisquick*®
¾	cup old-fashioned oats, *Quaker*®
½	cup slivered almonds, *Diamond*®
2	tablespoons butter, melted

1. Combine apple pie filling, rhubarb, brown sugar, sugar, cinnamon, tapioca, apple juice, and lemon juice in a 4-quart slow cooker. Stir thoroughly.

2. Cover and cook on HIGH setting for 2 to 3 hours.

3. For crisp topping, preheat oven to 350 degrees F one half hour before serving. Line a baking sheet with aluminum foil and set aside.

4. In a small bowl, combine crisp topping ingredients. Spread on prepared baking sheet and bake for 12 to 14 minutes or until golden brown. Sprinkle crisp topping over warm apple rhubarb.

Rice Pudding with Dried Apricots

Prep 10 minutes
Cook Low 2 to 4 hours
Servings 8

Butter-flavored cooking spray
1   can (12-ounce) evaporated milk, *Carnation®*
1   can (14-ounce) sweetened condensed milk, *Carnation®*
4   large eggs
1   teaspoon salt
2   bags (8.8 ounces each) uncooked long grain ready rice, *Uncle Ben's®*
2   tablespoons crystallized ginger, *The Spice Hunter®*
1   bag (6-ounce) dried apricots, *Sunsweet®*

1. Spray the inside of a 4-or 5-quart slow cooker with cooking spray.

2. In a large bowl, whisk together evaporated milk, condensed milk, eggs, and salt. Stir in rice, crystallized ginger, and dried apricots. Pour into slow cooker.

3. Cover and cook on LOW setting for 2 to 4 hours.

Banana Chocolate Chip Cake

Prep 15 minutes
Cook Low 4 to 5 hours
Servings 10

Butter-flavored cooking spray
½ cup mashed ripe bananas
2 tablespoons hazelnut liqueur, *Frangelico®*
1 box (15.5-ounce) banana nut muffin mix, *Betty Crocker®*
½ cup evaporated milk, *Carnation®*
2 tablespoons vegetable oil, *Crisco®*
1 egg
1 teaspoon vanilla extract, *McCormick®*
1 teaspoon cinnamon
½ cup semisweet chocolate chips
1 teaspoon rum extract, *McCormick®*
1 can (16-ounce) cream cheese frosting, *Betty Crocker®*
1 cup chopped walnuts, *Diamond®*

1. Spray bottom of a 1½-quart soufflé dish with butter-flavored cooking spray. Line bottom of soufflé dish with parchment paper and give a quick spray with cooking spray. Make a foil ring, 1-inch thick, for soufflé dish to sit on inside a 5-quart slow cooker.

2. In medium bowl, combine bananas with hazelnut liqueur. Add muffin mix, evaporated milk, oil, egg, vanilla extract, cinnamon, and chocolate chips. Stir together until just blended.

3. Transfer to prepared soufflé dish. Place dish on top of foil ring in slow cooker. Lay 8 paper towels over top of slow cooker bowl and secure with lid. (This helps to trap steam.) Cook on LOW setting for 4 to 5 hours.

4. Remove cake and allow to cool completely.

5. Cut cake in half horizontally. Stir rum extract into cream cheese frosting and frost in between layers and outside of cake with mixture.

6. Garnish side of cake with chopped walnuts.

Oaxacan Mango Compote

Prep 5 minutes
Cook High 3 to 4 hours
Servings 8

2	bags (12 ounces each) frozen mango chunks, *Kern's*®
1	bag (4-ounce) dried mango, chopped, *Marianni*®
½	cup orange tequila, *Jose Cuervo*®
½	cup mango nectar, *Kern's*®
¼	cup brown sugar, *C&H*®
1	tablespoon chili powder, *Gebhardt's*®
1	pinch cayenne, or more if desired

1. Combine all ingredients in a 4-or 5-quart slow cooker. Stir thoroughly.

2. Cover and cook on HIGH setting for 3 to 4 hours.

Serving ideas: Delicious over coconut sorbet or Jell-O Flan (3.0 ounces) made with ½ teaspoon lemon extract.

Caramel-Toffee Apples

Prep 15 minutes
Cook Low 1½ to 2 hours
Servings 10

These luscious little morsels take you right back to childhood. Served bite size, they make a delightful indulgence, or wrap a whole apple in cellophane and tie with a ribbon to make a scrumptious gift.

2	bags (14 ounces each) caramel candies, unwrapped, *Kraft*®
¼	cup apple juice, *Tree Top*®
½	teaspoon pumpkin pie spice, *McCormick*®
2	bags (14 ounces each) sliced green apples, *Chiquita*®
2	bags (8 ounces each) toffee bits, *Heath*®

1. Place unwrapped caramels, apple juice, and pumpkin pie spice in a 4-quart slow cooker. Cover and cook on LOW setting for 1½ to 2 hours, stirring every 15 minutes.

2. Pour toffee bits onto a rimmed baking sheet. Insert a fork into an apple slice. Dip, skin only, into caramel then roll in toffee bits until well coated.

3. Lay on parchment paper to cool. Repeat until all ingredients are used.

Serving Ideas: To make whole Caramel Apples, insert a popsicle stick into the center of a whole apple. Dip into caramel then roll in toffee bits. Place on parchment paper to cool.

Island Bread Pudding

Prep 10 minutes
Cook Low 3 to 4 hours
Servings 6

Cubed Hawaiian bread is the base for this ambrosial treat flavored with coconut, pineapple, and cinnamon. The heat releases the sweetness in the dark rum, caramelizing it into a satiny glaze. Dried tropical fruits add confetti color.

	Butter-flavored cooking spray
1	pound Hawaiian Bread, cut into 1-inch cubes, *King's*®
1	cup pineapple chunks, drained, *Dole*®
1	bag (7-ounce) dried tropical fruit trio, *Sun-Maid*®
1	can (12-ounce) coconut milk, *Thai Kitchen*®
¼	cup dark rum, *Myer's*®
1	cup pineapple-coconut nectar, *Kern's*®
1	cup brown sugar, *C&H*®
3	large eggs
¼	teaspoon cinnamon
½	teaspoon salt
2	tablespoons butter, cut into small pieces

1. Spray the inside of a 4-or 5-quart slow cooker with butter-flavored cooking spray.

2. In a large bowl, combine bread cubes, pineapple, and dried tropical mix.

3. In a medium bowl, whisk together coconut milk, rum, nectar, sugar, eggs, cinnamon, and salt. Pour over bread mixture. Stir until mixture is well combined and bread is saturated. Transfer to slow cooker. Dot with butter.

4. Cover and cook on LOW setting for 3 to 4 hours.

Bananas Foster on Oatmeal-Rum Cookies

Prep 10 minutes
Cook High 1 hour
Servings 8

FOR BANANAS FOSTER
- 6   bananas, peeled, cut into ½-inch diagonal slices
- ½   cup light brown sugar, *C&H*®
- ½   cup dark rum, *Myer's*®
- ½   teaspoon pumpkin pie spice, *McCormick*®

FOR OATMEAL-RUM COOKIES
- 1   package (17.5-ounce) oatmeal cookie mix, *Betty Crocker*®
- 1   stick butter, softened
- 1   large egg
- 1   tablespoon dark rum, *Myer's*®
- 2   teaspoons rum extract. *McCormick*®
-     Vanilla ice cream, for serving

1. In a 4 or 5-quart slow cooker, combine all Bananas Foster ingredients and toss well.

2. Cover and cook on HIGH setting for 1 hour.

3. For the oatmeal-rum cookies, preheat oven to 375 degrees F. In a large bowl, combine all Oatmeal-Rum Cookie ingredients. Mix into a stiff dough.

4. Drop two tablespoons of cookie dough, two inches apart, onto ungreased baking sheet. Bake for 10 to 12 minutes. Remove cookies and let cool completely. Repeat until all cookies are baked.

Serving ideas: Spoon ice cream over cookies and top with bananas foster.

Blackberry-Peach Betty

Prep 10 minutes
Cook Low 3 to 4 hours
Servings 6

You seldom see blackberries and peaches served together—a shame, because the vivid contrast of colors and sweet-and-tangy tastes makes a lively dessert. Straight-from-the-box graham crackers cook into a readymade crust.

	Butter-flavored cooking spray
1	can (21-ounce) peach pie filling, *Comstock More Fruit*®
1	bag (16-ounce) frozen blackberries, *Dole*®
¼	cup granulated sugar
1	teaspoon cinnamon
1	cup graham crackers (about 6 to 8 crackers), crushed, *Honey Maid*®
6	tablespoons butter, cut into small pieces

1. Spray a 4-quart slow cooker with butter-flavored cooking spray.

2. In a medium bowl, combine peach pie filling, blackberries, sugar, and cinnamon. Pour half of fruit mixture into slow cooker. Top with half of the crushed graham crackers. Dot with half of the butter. Repeat layers with remaining ingredients.

3. Cover and cook on LOW setting for 3 to 4 hours.

Serving ideas: Great à la mode with a scoop of vanilla ice cream or a dollop of whipped topping.

Crème de Menthe Brownies

Prep 15 minutes
Cook Low 4½ to 6 hours
Servings 12

	Butter-flavored cooking spray
1	box (19.5-ounce) milk chocolate brownie mix, *Pillsbury*®
3	eggs, divided
½	cup vegetable oil, *Crisco*®
¼	cup Crème de Menthe
½	cup Crème de Menthe thins (about 18), chopped, *Andes*®
1	block (8-ounce) cream cheese, softened, *Philadelphia*®
½	cup granulated sugar
½	teaspoon mint extract, *McCormick*®

1. Lightly spray a 1½-quart soufflé dish with butter-flavored cooking spray. Line bottom of soufflé dish with parchment paper and give another quick spray. Make a foil ring, 1-inch thick, for soufflé dish to sit on inside a 5-quart slow cooker.

2. In a medium bowl, combine brownie mix, two eggs, vegetable oil, Crème de Menthe, and chopped mint thins. Stir 50 strokes to combine. Transfer to prepared soufflé dish.

3. In a medium bowl, combine cream cheese, remaining egg, sugar, and mint extract. Using an electric mixer beat on low speed until smooth. Spread over brownie mixture. Use a butter knife to cut cream cheese mixture into brownie mixture for a marble effect.

4. Place soufflé dish on top of foil ring in slow cooker. Lay 8 paper towels over top of slow cooker bowl and secure with lid. (This helps to trap steam.) Cook on LOW setting for 4½ to 6 hours. (Do not lift lid to check brownies for the first 3 hours.)

Tip: Allow brownies to cool completely before cutting.

Mexican Hot Chocolate

Prep 10 minutes
Cook Low 2 to 3 hours
Servings 8

Go ahead, drink dessert. Dark chocolate is brewed to perfection with aromatic warming spices like cinnamon and nutmeg. Serve it in an Irish coffee mug with a cloud of whipped cream, so all can admire its velvety presentation.

6	cans (12 ounces each) evaporated milk, *Carnation*®
4	teaspoons cinnamon
1	tablespoon vanilla extract, *McCormick*®
1	teaspoon nutmeg
2	bags (12 ounces each) dark chocolate chips, *Hershey's*®
	Whipped topping for serving, *Cool Whip*®
	Cocoa powder for serving, *Hershey's*®

1. In a 4-quart slow cooker, whisk together milk, cinnamon, vanilla extract, and nutmeg. Add chocolate chips.

2. Cover and cook on LOW setting for 2 to 3 hours, stirring every 15 to 20 Minutes.

Serving ideas: Serve with a dollop of whipped topping and a dusting of cocoa powder.

Party Food

They're easy to make and easy to eat—that's why snack foods are forever in vogue. In the 1980s, I served wine coolers, Brie, and fondue scooped out of crusty bread bowls. The 1990s brought bruschetta, mesquite-smoked pizza, and designer beer. The turn of the millennium ushered in the sleek sophistication of 'tinis and tapas. And today, I use that 1970s slow cooker to bring them all together in a fun finger food buffet that's party-ready, pronto.

This chapter serves up a smorgasbord of little dishes with big taste, from dips to dim sum to crudités. Having a get-together? Welcome guests with stylish starters, like Caramelized Onions and Apples over Brie. Turn munchies into a mini meal with Thai Chicken Meatballs or Guava Chili Baby Back Ribs. Pour on the happy hour ambiance with Chai Tea Toddies, and then send guests home with a smile by serving a classy Café à l'Orange that's rich enough to double as dessert.

The Recipes

Thai Chicken Meatballs in Red Curry Sauce

Prep 20 minutes
Cook Low 4 to 6 hours
Makes 48 (1-inch) meatballs

FOR CHICKEN MEATBALLS
- 2 **pounds ground chicken**
- ½ **cup fresh chopped cilantro**
- 1 **tablespoon salt-free Thai seasoning,** *The Spice Hunter®*
- 1 **teaspoon crushed garlic,** *Christopher Ranch®*
- 2 **tablespoons soy sauce,** *Kikkoman®*
- 2 **tablespoons lime juice,** *ReaLime®*
- 1 **cup bread crumbs,** *Progresso®*

FOR RED CURRY SAUCE
- 1 **can (14-ounce) coconut milk,** *Thai Kitchen®*
- 1 **bottle (8-ounce) clam juice,** *Snow's®*
- 2 **tablespoons lime juice,** *ReaLime®*
- 1 **tablespoon red curry paste,** *Thai Kitchen®*
- 2 **cups peeled and slivered red onion**

1. Preheat broiler. Line a heavy duty baking sheet with aluminum foil and set aside. In a large bowl, combine all meatball ingredients. Using a wooden spoon or clean hands, mix thoroughly. Shape into 1-inch balls.

2. Place meatballs on prepared baking sheet and broil 6 inches from heat source for 8 to10 minutes, turning once.

3. Whisk together all sauce ingredients in a medium bowl, except slivered onions. Set aside. Place half of the slivered onions in the bottom of a 5-quart slow cooker. Add several meatballs at a time to the bowl of sauce. Coat meatballs with sauce and transfer to slow cooker using a slotted spoon. Repeat until all meatballs are well coated. Pour remaining sauce over meatballs and sprinkle with remaining slivered onions.

4. Cover and cook on LOW setting for 4 to 6 hours. Strain and defat the cooking liquid. Serve as sauce on the side. Garnish with fresh cilantro.

Tip: Occasionally wet hands with cold water when making meatballs. This will prevent sticking.

Sweet and Sour Porkballs

Prep 15 minutes
Cook Low 4 to 6 hours
Makes 48 (1-inch) meatballs

FOR MEATBALLS
- 2 pounds ground pork
- 1 can (8-ounce) crushed pineapple, *Dole®*
- 1 tablespoon soy sauce, *Kikkoman®*
- 1 tablespoon Szechwan seasoning, *McCormick®*
- ½ cup frozen chopped green peppers, *Pictsweet®*
- 2 scallions, chopped
- ¼ cup bread crumbs, *Progresso®*

FOR SWEET AND SOUR SAUCE
- 1 packet (2⅛-ounce) sweet & sour sauce mix, *Kikkoman®*
- ¼ cup rice vinegar
- 2 cans (6 ounces each) pineapple juice, *Dole®*
- ¼ cup tomato paste, *Contadina®*
- ½ cup apricot-pineapple preserves, *Smucker's®*

1. Preheat broiler. Line a heavy duty baking sheet with aluminum foil and set aside. In a large bowl, combine all meatball ingredients and using a wooden spoon or clean hands mix thoroughly. Shape into 1-inch balls.

2. Place meatballs on prepared baking sheet and broil 6 inches from the heat source for 8 to 10 minutes, turning once.

3. For sauce whisk together all sauce ingredients in a large bowl. Add several meatballs at a time to the bowl of sauce. Coat meatballs with sauce and transfer to a 5-quart slow cooker using a slotted spoon. Repeat until all meatballs are well coated. Pour remaining sauce over meatballs.

4. Cover and cook on LOW setting for 4 to 6 hours. Strain and defat the cooking liquid. Serve as sauce on the side.

Meatballs in Chipotle Sauce

Prep 15 minutes
Cook Low 4 to 6 hours
Makes 48 (1-inch) meatballs

1	pound ground pork
1	pound ground beef
2	tablespoons fresh chopped cilantro
⅓	cup frozen chopped onions, *Ore-Ida®*
1	tablespoon salt-free Mexican seasoning, *The Spice Hunter®*
1	large egg
¼	cup bread crumbs, *Progresso®*
2	jars (16 ounces each) salsa verde, *La Victoria®*
2	packets (1.25 ounces each) smokey chipotle taco seasoning mix, *Ortega®*
¼	cup gold tequila, *Jose Cuervo®*
	fresh chopped cilantro for garnish (optional)

1. Preheat broiler. Line a heavy duty baking sheet with aluminum foil and set aside.

2. In a large bowl, combine first seven ingredients. Using a wooden spoon or clean hands mix thoroughly. Shape into 1-inch balls. Place meatballs on prepared baking sheet, evenly spaced, and broil 6 inches from heat source for 8 to 10 minutes, turning once. Remove from oven and set aside.

3. In a large bowl, combine salsa verde, taco seasoning, and tequila. Stir and pour ¼ of the sauce into the bottom of a 5-quart slow cooker. Add several meatballs at a time to the bowl, coating them with sauce. Transfer to slow cooker using a slotted spoon. Repeat until all meatballs are well coated. Pour remaining sauce over meatballs.

4. Cover and cook on LOW setting for 4 to 6 hours. Strain and defat the cooking liquid. Serve as sauce on the side. Garnish with fresh cilantro.

Cider Ribs

Prep 15 minutes
Cook Low 6 to 8 hours
Servings 12

These lively pork ribs are a twist on traditional Carolina BBQ, with a tangy vinegar base made even tangier with fermented apple. Spiced apple cider, sweet apple juice, and tart apple cider vinegar add delicious dimension to the hickory smoke.

2	packets (.74 ounces each) spiced apple cider drink mix, *Alpine*®
1	packet (1.25-ounce) mild chili seasoning, *McCormick*®
2	racks pork baby back ribs, rinsed and patted dry
1½	cups Hickory Smoke BBQ Sauce, *Bull's-Eye*®
¼	cup frozen apple juice concentrate, *Tree Top*®
¼	cup apple cider vinegar, *Heinz*®

1. Preheat broiler. Line a heavy duty baking sheet with aluminum foil and set aside. In a large bowl, combine apple cider drink mix and chili seasoning. Set aside.

2. Slice ribs into single-bone portions. Dredge ribs in cider and seasoning mixture and place on prepared baking sheet, meaty side up. Broil 6 inches from heat source for 10 to 12 minutes. Turn and broil additional 10 to 12 minutes.

3. Transfer ribs to a 5-quart slow cooker, meat side up.

4. In a small bowl, combine remaining ingredients and pour sauce over ribs. Cover and cook on LOW setting for 6 to 8 hours. Strain and defat the cooking liquid. Serve as sauce on the side.

Guava Chili Baby Back Ribs

Prep 15 minutes
Cook Low 6 to 8 hours
Servings 12

2	racks pork baby back ribs, rinsed and patted dry
1	packet (1.25-ounce) mild chili seasoning, *McCormick®*
1	jar (8.5-ounce) guava jelly, *Margie's®*
1	can (6-ounce) tomato paste, *Contadina®*
1	cup guava nectar, *Kern's®*
¼	cup dark rum, *Myer's®*
3	tablespoons lime juice, *ReaLime®*

1. Preheat broiler. Line a heavy duty baking sheet with aluminum foil and set aside.

2. Slice ribs into single-bone portions. Rub ribs with chili seasoning mix and place on prepared baking sheet, meaty side up. Broil 6 inches from heat source for 10 to 12 minutes. Turn and broil for additional 10 to 12 minutes.

3. In a large bowl, whisk together remaining ingredients. Place ribs in a 5-quart slow cooker, meat side up. Pour sauce over ribs. Cover and cook on LOW setting for 6 to 8 hours.

4. Remove ribs from slow cooker and cover to keep warm. Transfer sauce to a small saucepan. Bring to a boil over high heat and reduce by half. Remove from heat. (The sauce will thicken further as it cools.)

Serving ideas: Pass bowls of extra guava-infused sauce for dipping.

Rancher Ribs

Prep 15 minutes
Cook Low 6 to 8 hours
Servings 12

2	racks pork baby back ribs, rinsed and patted dry
1	tablespoon Montreal steak seasoning, *McCormick Grill Mates*®
1	cup BBQ sauce, *Bull's Eye*®
1	cup chili sauce, *Heinz*®
1	envelope (1.0-ounce) onion soup mix, *Lipton*®
¼	cup yellow mustard, *French's*®
2	tablespoons apple cider vinegar, *Heinz*®
½	cup molasses, *Grandma's*®
2	jalapeños, seeded, veined, and diced

1. Preheat broiler. Line heavy duty baking sheet with aluminum foil and set aside.

2. Slice ribs into single-bone portions. Rub ribs with Montreal steak seasoning and place on prepared baking sheet, meat side up. Broil 6 inches from heat source for 10 to 12 minutes. Turn and broil for an additional 10 to 12 minutes.

3. In a large bowl, stir together remaining ingredients. Using tongs, coat ribs, several at a time, with the sauce and coat thoroughly. Place in a 5-quart slow cooker. Repeat until all ribs are well coated. Pour remaining sauce over ribs.

4. Cover and cook on LOW setting for 6 to 8 hours. Strain and defat the cooking liquid. Serve as sauce on the side.

Jerked Chicken Wings

Prep 15 minutes
Cook High 2½ to 3½ hours
Servings 12

2½   pounds chicken drumettes, rinsed and patted dry
1   tablespoon salt-free chicken seasoning, *McCormick Grill Mates®*
1   cup chili sauce, *Heinz®*
½   cup pineapple juice, *Dole®*
¼   cup light brown sugar
1   tablespoon Jamaican Jerk seasoning, *McCormick®*
1   Habanero chile, seeded, veined, and diced

1. Preheat broiler. Line a heavy duty baking sheet with aluminum foil and set aside.

2. Season drumettes with chicken seasoning and place on prepared baking sheet. Broil 6 inches from heat source for 8 to 10 minutes, turning once.

3. In a large bowl, combine remaining ingredients. Using tongs, coat browned drumettes several at a time with sauce. Repeat until all drumettes are well coated. Place in a 5-quart slow cooker. Pour remaining sauce over drumettes.

4. Cover and cook on HIGH setting for 2½ to 3½ hours. Remove drumettes from slow cooker and tent with foil to keep warm. Strain and defat the cooking liquid. Serve as sauce on the side.

Tip: When working with habanero chiles, take extra precautions not to touch your eyes while handling these incendiary peppers. Wash hands frequently, or put on rubber gloves before chopping them.

Bandito Wings

Prep 15 minutes
Cook High 2½ to 3½ hours
Servings 12

2½   pounds chicken drumettes, rinsed and patted dry
1   tablespoon Montreal steak seasoning, *McCormick Grill Mates*®
¾   cup jalapeño jelly, *Knott's Berry Farm*®
½   cup chili sauce, *Heinz*®
2   tablespoons Tex-Mex chili seasoning, *McCormick*®
3   tablespoons diced jalapeños, *Ortega*®

1. Preheat broiler. Line a heavy duty baking sheet with aluminum foil and set aside. Season drumettes with steak seasoning and place on prepared baking sheet. Broil 6 inches from heat source for 8 to 10 minutes, turning once.

2. In a large bowl, whisk together remaining ingredients. Using tongs, coat drumettes several at a time with sauce. Repeat until all drumettes are well coated. Place in a 4 or 5-quart slow cooker. Pour remaining sauce over drumettes.

3. Cover and cook on HIGH setting for 2½ to 3½ hours.

Blackberry Wings

Prep 15 minutes
Cook High 2½ to 3½ hours
Sevings 12

Blackberry preserves and Pad Thai seasoning elevate happy hour drumettes to fine dining status. The prickly sweet heat of the Asian-inspired sauce works with any cut of chicken or pork to bring out the sweetness of the meat.

2½   pounds chicken drumettes, rinsed and patted dry
1   packet (1-ounce) Pad Thai seasoning mix, *Kikkoman*®
1   jar (16-ounce) blackberry preserves, *Knott's Berry Farm*®
¼   cup Dijon mustard, *Grey Poupon*®
1   tablespoon fresh chopped cilantro, plus more for garnish

1. Preheat broiler. Line a heavy duty baking sheet with aluminum foil and set aside.

2. In a large bowl, toss together drumettes and Pad Thai mix until chicken is thoroughly coated. Place on prepared baking sheet. Broil 6 inches from heat source for 8 to 10 minutes, turning once.

3. In a large bowl, combine blackberry preserves and Dijon mustard. Using tongs, coat drumettes several at a time with blackberry mustard mixture. Repeat until all drumettes are well coated.

4. Place in a 5-quart slow cooker. Pour remaining mixture over drumettes. Sprinkle with cilantro. Cover and cook on HIGH setting for 2½ to 3½ hours.

Queso con Tequila

Prep 5 minutes
Cook Low 3 to 4 hours
Servings: 16

Start with spunky pepper jack soup, stir in mounds of cream cheese and salsa, spike with a shot of tequila, and you've got a cheesaholic's delight. Serve it with chips for an appetizer or pour it over a baked potato for a colorful Tex-Mex meal.

2	cans (10 ounces each) condensed Southwest-style pepper jack soup, *Campbell's*®
1	pound pepper jack cheese, shredded, *Tillamook*®
2	packages (8 ounces each) cream cheese, cut into cubes, *Philadelphia*®
½	cup chunky salsa, *Newman's Own*®
¼	cup gold tequila, *Jose Cuervo*®
	Fresh cilantro, chopped, for garnish

1. In a 4-quart slow cooker, combine all ingredients, except cilantro, and mix thoroughly.

2. Cover and cook on LOW setting for 3 to 4 hours, stirring occasionally.

3. Stir and serve hot, garnished with fresh chopped cilantro.

Serving ideas: Serve with tortilla chips. Also tastes great over baked potatoes.

Hot Crab Rangoon Dip

Prep 5 minutes
Cook Low 2 to 3 hours
Servings 12

This rich, make-at-home dip has all the flavor of restaurant Rangoon, without the bother of stuffing and wrapping. Fry won tons into flat chips for dipping and serve with side bowls of hot mustard and sweet-and-sour sauce for added zing.

2	packages (8 ounces each) cream cheese, cut into cubes, *Philadelphia®*
2	cans (6 ounces each) lump crabmeat, drained and shredded, *Crown Prince®*
1	can (10-ounce) condensed shrimp bisque, *Campbell's®*
1	teaspoon Worcestershire sauce
2	teaspoons lemon juice, *ReaLemon®*
2	teaspoons soy sauce, *Kikkoman®*
1	scallion, finely chopped

1. In a 3-or 4-quart slow cooker combine all ingredients, and mix thoroughly.

2. Cover and cook on LOW setting for 2 to 3 hours, stirring occasionally.

Serving Ideas: Lightly fry won ton wrappers in peanut oil for dipping.

Spicy Cashew Dip

Prep 5 minutes
Cook Low 2 to 3 hours
Servings 12

2	packages (8 ounces each) cream cheese, *Philadelphia®*
1	cup unsalted cashew pieces, coarsely chopped
½	cup creamy peanut butter, *Skippy®*
2	tablespoons chili paste, Sambal Oelek
1	teaspoon curry powder, *Spice Islands®*
¾	cup coconut milk, *Thai Kitchen®*
1	tablespoon lime juice, *ReaLime®*
¼	cup finely chopped fresh cilantro, for garnish

1. In a 4-quart slow cooker, combine all ingredients except lime juice and cilantro, and mix thoroughly.

2. Cover and cook on LOW setting for 2 to 3 hours, stirring occasionally.

3. Stir in lime juice and serve hot garnished with cilantro.

Serving ideas: Serve with pre-sliced vegetables or packaged crudite platter sold at your local grocery store.

Tip: For a spicier dip, substitute hot curry powder for the milder variety used in this recipe.

Caramelized Onions and Apples with Brie

Prep 20 minutes
Cook Low 12 hours
Servings 12

2   large sweet onions, peeled and sliced into thick rounds
2   packages (14 ounces each) sliced green apples, *Chiquita*®
1   packet (1.8-ounce) white sauce mix, *Knorr*®
½   cup golden raisins, *Sun-Maid*®
⅓   cup light brown sugar
1   tablespoon Fines Herbes, *Spice Islands*®
1   stick butter, cut into small pieces
1   sheet puff pastry sheet, *Pepperidge Farm*®
1   wheel (13.2-ounce) baby brie, *Alouette*®

1. In a large bowl, combine onions, apples, white sauce mix, raisins, brown sugar, and Fines Herbes and toss well. Place mixture in a 5-quart slow cooker and dot with butter. Cover and cook on LOW setting for 12 hours.

2. A half hour before serving, preheat oven to 400 degrees F. Spray a heavy duty baking sheet with nonstick cooking spray and set aside.

3. Unroll pastry sheet from package and lay flat. Place brie wheel in the center of puff pastry and wrap cheese by bringing ends of pastry together toward the center of the wheel. Carefully turn wheel over, folding pastry ends under securely. Lay on prepared baking sheet, fold side down. Bake for 25 minutes until light golden brown. Let cool 10 minutes.

4. Top pastry wrapped brie with caramelized onions and apple mixture, and serve warm.

Wild Mushroom Dip

Prep 20 minutes
Cook Low 3 to 4 hours
Servings 12

2	cups white wine, Chardonnay
2	containers (.5 ounces each) dried wild mushrooms, mixed variety, *Ready Pac®**
2	packages (8 ounces each) cream cheese, cut into cubes, *Philadelphia®*
2	cans (10¾ ounces each) condensed cream of mushroom soup, *Campbell's®*
2	cups shredded mozzarella, *Sargento®*
1	teaspoon dried tarragon
1	teaspoon salt
½	teaspoon ground black pepper

1. In a microwave-safe bowl, heat white wine in microwave oven on HIGH for 3 to 5 minutes. Place dried mushrooms in wine and let sit for 10 minutes to rehydrate.

2. Strain mushrooms through a fine mesh sieve set over a bowl, and reserve liquid. Transfer mushrooms to a food processor. Puree to a coarse paste consistency.

3. In a large bowl, combine mushroom paste, ⅔ cup reserved mushroom liquid, and remaining ingredients. Mix thoroughly and pour into a 4-quart slow cooker.

4. Cover and cook on LOW setting for 3 to 4 hours, stirring once halfway through.

Serving ideas: Serve with crustry bread, cut into cubes.

*Pre-packaged dried wild mushrooms are found in the produce department of your local grocery store.

Guinness Cheddar Fondue

Prep 5 minutes
Cook Low 3 to 4 hours
Servings 12

2   cans (10 ounces each) condensed cheddar soup, *Campbell's*®
2   teaspoons Worcestershire sauce
1   teaspoon garlic juice, *McCormick*®
1   teaspoon dry English mustard, *Colman's*®
1   bottle (12-ounce) *Guinness Stout*®
1   pound (4 cups) shredded cheddar cheese, *Kraft*®

1. In a 4-quart slow cooker, combine all ingredients and mix thoroughly.

2. Cover and cook on LOW setting for 3 to 4 hours, stirring occasionally. Serve hot.

Serving ideas: Serve with 1-pound loaf of dense whole grain bread cut into cubes.

Peach and Apricot Hard Cider

Prep 5 minutes
Cook Low 2 to 3 hours
Serves 10

2	cans (11.5 ounces each) peach nectar, *Kern's*®
2	cans (11.5 ounces each) apricot nectar, *Kern's*®
1	bag (12-ounce) frozen peach slices, *Dole*®
3	cups water
1	cup whiskey
½	cup lemon juice, *ReaLemon*®
1	cup light brown sugar
1	teaspoon ground allspice
2 to 3	cinnamon sticks, plus more for garnish

1. In a 4-quart slow cooker, combine all ingredients. Cover and cook on LOW setting for 2 to 3 hours.

2. Remove cinnamon sticks and switch to WARM setting for serving.

Serving ideas: Serve in Irish coffee mugs with a cinnamon stick swizzle.

Cafe à l'Orange

Prep 5 minutes
Cook Low 2 to 3 hours
Serves 12

6	cups water
6	tablespoons instant coffee crystals, *Folgers*®
½	cup chocolate liqueur, *Godiva*®
½	cup orange liqueur, *Grand Marnier*®
2	tablespoons cocoa powder, plus more for garnish, *Hershey's*®
⅔	cup granulated sugar
2	cups half-and-half
1	container (8-ounce) whipped topping, *Cool Whip*®
1	teaspoon orange extract
2	oranges, sliced

1. In a 4-quart slow cooker, stir together water, instant coffee, both liqueurs, cocoa powder, and sugar. Cover and cook on LOW setting for 2 to 3 hours.

2. Stir in half-and-half and switch to WARM setting. Stir orange extract into whipped topping.

3. Serve in Irish coffee mugs with a dollop of orange flavored whipped topping and a dusting of cocoa powder. Garnish each glass with a slice of fresh orange.

Chai Tea Toddy

Prep 5 minutes
Cook Low 2 hours, **Warm** for serving
Servings 10

Splash in some spiced rum, vanilla vodka, and condensed milk and this ancient Indian secret becomes a festive cocktail you can savor anywhere. Garnish with a cinnamon stick stirrer, sit back, and revel in the instant pleasure it brings.

8	cups boiling water
16	bags Chai Black Tea, *Stash*®
½	cup spiced rum, *Captain Morgan*®
½	cup vanilla vodka, *Stoli Vanil*®
2	cinnamon sticks, plus more for serving
2	cups sweetened condensed milk, *Eagle Brand*®

1. Pour boiling water into a 4-quart slow cooker. Place tea bags in slow cooker and secure lid with tea bag tabs hanging outside. Let steep for 10 minutes. Remove tea bags and discard.

2. Stir in rum and vodka. Add cinnamon sticks. Cover and cook on LOW setting for 2 hours.

3. Stir in condensed milk and switch to WARM setting for serving.

Serving ideas: Serve in Irish coffee mugs with cinnamon stick swizzles.

Index

Index

Free

Lifestyle web magazine subscription

Just visit

www.semi-homemade.com

today to subscribe!

Sign yourself and your friends and family up to the semi-homemaker's club today!

Each online issue is filled with fast, easy how-to projects, simple lifestyle solutions, and an abundance of helpful hints and terrific tips. It's the complete go-to magazine for busy people on-the-move.

tables & settings   fashion & beauty   ideas   home & garden   fabulous florals

super suppers   perfect parties   great gatherings   decadent desserts

gifts & giving   details   wines & music   fun favors   semi-homemaker's club

Semi-Homemade.com

making life easier, better, and more enjoyable

Semihomemade.com has hundreds of ways to simplify your life—the easy Semi-Homemade way! You'll find fast ways to de-clutter, try your hand at clever crafts, create terrific tablescapes or decorate indoors and out to make your home and garden superb with style.

We're especially proud of our Semi-Homemakers club: a part of semi-homemade.com which hosts other semihomemakers just like you. The club community shares ideas to make life easier, better, and more manageable with smart tips and hints allowing you time to do what you want! Sign-up and join today—it's free—and sign up your friends and family, too! It's easy the Semi-Homemade way! Visit the site today and start enjoying your busy life!

*Sign yourself and your friends and family up
to the semi-homemaker's club today!*

tablescapes   home   garden   organizing   crafts

everyday & special days   cooking   entertaining   cocktail time

Halloween   Thanksgiving   Christmas   Valentine's   Easter   New Year's

Sandra Lee
Semi-Homemade® Cookbook Series

Collect all these smartly helpful, timesaving, and beautiful books!

Find even more sensible, savvy solutions online at semihomemade.com.

Look for the series wherever quality books are sold.